How to Blow Up Your Business in 2019

The Go-To Guide to Scale Your Brand to New Heights with Social Media Marketing, Facebook Advertising, Internet Funnels and More! (Digital Marketing for Beginners)

Written by Elliott Jaworski

purposes only. All effort has been executed to present accurate, up to date, and reliable, complete information. No warranties of any kind are declared or implied. Readers acknowledge that the author is not engaging in the rendering of legal, financial, medical or professional advice. The content within this book has been derived from various sources. Please consult a licensed professional before attempting any techniques outlined in this book.

By reading this document, the reader agrees that under no circumstances is the author responsible for any losses, direct or indirect, which are incurred as a result of the use of information contained within this document, including, but not limited to, — errors, omissions, or inaccuracies.

Table of Contents

Introduction

A lot of businesses in the current world, whether big or small, carry out internet marketing. Why is this so? This is the fastest and most economical way of reaching millions of your target market. Internet marketing is also referred to as online marketing and it involves the promotion of a brand, products, or services via the internet. Internet marketing is broad as it includes email marketing, electronic relationship management, as well as any promotional activities that are done via wireless media.

This book will teach you how to change with the times, and be relevant in the world of internet marketing. We live in a dynamic world, and in this case, the internet world where things are rapidly changing. Different people react to situations differently. Some are resistant to change, some are so surprised with changes that they can't do anything to salvage the situation while others adapt to change and make everything work. This book will teach you how to be the one who can discover how to deal with change, so that you can enjoy the success that comes with internet marketing.

We look at three kinds of people when it comes to digital marketing:

- Those who realize change early

- Those who rush into action

- Those who resist change and believe it will lead to something worse

- Those who learn to adapt with time when change happens

No matter what kind of person you are, we all have one common denominator which is finding our way through the maze of internet marketing. Consequently, the purpose of this book is to help you find your way in internet marketing.

We all know that achieving success makes us happy and holding on to what makes us happy is often difficult. However, the fact is that if you fail to change with the modern trends in internet marketing, you will become obsolete and irrelevant. You need to realize that you can achieve better things if you only overcame your fear of the unknown.

For you to be successful in digital marketing, you need to let go of old beliefs and ways of internet marketing. Therefore, move with the trends. The purpose of this book is to help you find new ways of being successful and developing new ways in internet marketing.

Chapter 1 : Instagram Marketing

For a while now, Instagram has been gaining traction. Everyone is talking about it, and its use is the in thing today, together with other networks like Snapchat and Twitter. It currently has over 800 million users all over the world. You must have at one point heard of it and may be wondering what it is all about.

Instagram is a photo album of sorts. Think of the time you went over to a friend's place and their family members pulled out a photo album from years back, and you could go through it to see their memories from that time. Those moments in life that you want to capture and show your friends, adding it to your album.

It is a social networking app whose sole purpose is to allow people to share images and videos from a smartphone. In essence, you get a virtual photo album to share with friends and family.

They can view your photos when you post them, and even comment about them on the app.

The app is available for use on mobile devices and computers although it works best with mobile devices. You can simply download it for free from the App Store for iOS, Google Play Store for Android devices, and Windows Phone Store for phones using the Windows OS.

If you are new to Instagram, it may look like rocket science with all the icons on it. Far from this, however, you will come to find that it is fairly easy to use once you get the hang of it.

How It Works

The first step in using Instagram is to download the app on the respective platform depending on the kind of device you are using.

Account Creation

You will need to create an account as the first step. To create your account, open the app on your mobile device and tap on the Sign-Up option. You will be prompted to enter your email address.

There is also the option of signing up with your Facebook account so that they are connected. It is on the same sign-up page, where you can either sign up or Log in with Facebook.

Once that is done, move on to the next step of creating passwords and a username. The username is what people will see when they see your posts. It usually appears on top of your post and your profile.

The username is the mode of recognition for Instagram users and is usually preceded by a symbol @. So, if you decide to name your account Greg17, it will look like this: @Greg17.

If you are opening a business account, go to settings on the app and select a business account. It will allow you to add more information such as a phone number for those who want to reach you, business hours, and an address, all to make it easier to find your store and interact with you.

The profile

Once you have created your account successfully, the next step is to set up your profile. This includes choosing a suitable profile photo which will represent you, adding your name and a small message that describes you, also referred to as a bio. You can also add a link to a website if you have one.

This part is important for businesses as it gives the audience more information about you and what you offer. It also helps to get more people to follow you as they will know a bit about you. For the profile photo, think of having your company logo so as to market your brand.

Once this step is done, you are officially a member of Instagram and can start right away viewing images of other members as well as following them and having them follow you back. You can always change the image and update information on your profile later.

Accessing Images from other Users

To be able to see images of friends and family, you will need to follow them. Simply search for their usernames and click on the follow button beside or below their names. Instagram also may give you a list of people you may know, and you can follow them too.

People will also be able to follow you to see images that you post. On your profile, you will see the following count, showing the number of people following you as well as the number of people you are following.

There is also a privacy setting that only allows those who follow you to see your images. If you come across the profile of an individual who has the privacy setting, you will not be able to view their images and videos until you follow them.

You can set your account to private or let it be open to the public according to your preferences. Having a private account lets you decide who you want to follow you as you can either accept or deny their request to follow you.

Interactions on Instagram

The app allows you to interact with others quite easily. You will have a profile and a newsfeed. On the profile, you will find information about you and the images and videos you have shared.

The newsfeed is where you will see posts by others that appear on a timeline. You can scroll to view images by other people. Here is where the interactions between you and the others occur. You can leave a comment on the images you view and like them.

You like a post by tapping on the heart shape at the bottom left corner of the image. Alternatively, you can double tap the image. It is quite a fun and interesting way to interact, as you can have conversations in the comment section.

It is easy, right?

Posting Photos

Click on the icon with a plus sign. This is where

you choose photos to add to your profile. You can either capture a photo or choose one from your device. Remember to pick a photo that is appealing and relevant.

Your account should look inviting to capture the interest of users and add them to your followers' list, so pick presentable photos that make this possible.

You will notice that you will not be attracted to users whose profiles are dull, thus you need to keep it interesting and creative.

The frequency of posting photos depends on the time you have, as well as the purpose of your posts. You can post as many times as you want since there are no limits to the number of images one can post.

Not posting for long periods of time may, however, make it hard to increase your following. Try to post every once in a while, to be relevant to other users.

Editing the Photos

Why does everyone look like a professional photographer on Instagram? You may wonder. Are they just very photogenic? Or did they all go to photography school? Well, maybe it's the good lighting. But chances are they may have only been making good use of the editing features offered on Instagram.

Once you choose a photo to post, you can click on the edit option where you can tweak the photo to your desire, by cropping it, trying out different filters to find which suits you most, and make other adjustments as you will.

The editing tools allow you to alter contrasts, have varying degrees of brightness, change the angle of your photos, or even add some blur to part of the image to make it more interesting. You can also try out different effects on the image. Discover your creativity with these changes and filters and find out how good your skills are.

Sharing Posts

Once you are satisfied with the chosen image or video, you can move to the next step. You are given the option of adding a caption to the image, tag friends, if they appear on the image or if you would like for them to be notified of it. You can also tag it to the geographic location it was taken or where you are at that moment and publish it.

Publishing means that it has been added to your profile, and it will appear on the newsfeeds of other users. They will also be able to like the image and leave comments on it.

There is the option of connecting your account with your other accounts on Facebook, Twitter, and the others, found in the configuration settings. Once you enable the settings, your images will be posted simultaneously on all the platforms you choose.

Instagram Stories

This particular feature was introduced to Instagram recently. You can add videos and images to your story just as a normal Instagram post. However, the images and videos posted on your story usually disappear after 24 hours.

They also do not appear on your profile. The stories usually appear at the top of your Instagram feed. You can tell them apart from regular newsfeeds as the ones that appear in small photo bubbles of people you follow.

Currently, Instagram stories do not have the option for one to like or comment on them. You can only view them.

Hashtags

You cannot speak on Instagram without mentioning hashtags. These usually assist users to discover posts on an area of interest for them. For instance, for a post about baking items, you can use the hashtag #Cake or #bakers. If you go to the explore section, you can search for a specific hashtag and it will bring you posts made with that hashtag.

For a business account, this particular part would

be important to put you on the map for users in search of something in your field.

Instagram is a fun app that lets you view amazing images. You can never see everything on it, with so many images being shared around. To find new images that interest you, just head on to the explore section and type in # followed by something that you would like to see.

You can also discover new people that you may follow by tapping on the search icon represented by a magnifying glass. This takes you to posts by users similar to those you follow and posts you have liked before.

Instagram is all about the visuals, catering to your sense of sight. If you are one who loves visuals, then you will love the app with its ability to bring to you art in different forms. It allows for communication and the exchange of ideas through the posts.

That is all there is to it. It is quite easy and straightforward to learn and interesting when you are able to use it. You will understand why people, especially the younger generation, spend hours on it.

How Instagram Works; The different functionalities

Now, we have a better understanding of what Instagram really is and what it is all about. With that information, we should be able to confidently use the app as marketers or business owners.

Whatever niche you are in, you can always use the app to market your product.

So, how does it work?

We have mentioned a few of the features in the previous chapter. We will then delve deeper into the different functionalities of the app and examine how the different features work and how you may use them effectively for Instagram marketing.

If you have been interested in using Instagram

for your marketing purposes but have no idea where to start, here is your chance. Let us break down the app for you in such a way that you understand it.

Instagram Features

There are several features on Instagram that you should know of to be able to use it well in marketing. It would be good to note that Instagram keeps changing with the times.

This means that the layout, as well as how it works may change, with newer ideas coming into play as the team behind Instagram works to upgrade the app and keep it relevant.

Let us look at some of the current features:

1. *Instagram Stories*

As previously discussed in Chapter 1, Instagram Stories is one feature that was introduced recently. It lets the user add photos or videos which usually last for 24 hours.

This particular feature is similar to Snapchat as the photos and videos posted there also tend to disappear after 24 hours.

Once you open the app on your mobile device, you will see bubbles or circles at the top of your newsfeed. These are the stories posted by people you follow.

You are not limited to viewing the posts once, but you can view them over and over until the 24 hours are up after which they vanish.

You can view an image for 10 seconds before the next image on the story pops up. Tapping on the image and holding allows you to view it for a while longer.

The feature lets you record live videos to post and add as many photos as you like to the story. Try it out, take an image or two of your products and add them to your story. This is a great way to promote your product using the feature.

Add relevant information to the image, possibly a

geotag to show the viewers the location of the physical store if there is one.

There is a count for your story that shows you the number of views, that way you can know how many people see your story, and know which stories have more viewers than others. This helps with future plans as you will understand what the viewers like. You also have the freedom to hide your story from some users, such that they won't see it in their feeds.

Want to leave a comment on an interesting image on someone's story?

Look at the bottom of your screen while viewing a story and click on the 'write a message' then proceed to type out your message. And if for one reason or other you want to stop a user from sending you private messages, you can leave them out of people who can send you direct messages.

For a business, this feature lets you create new and interactive live content for your audience.

You can have daily challenges, promotions, and other such ideas to keep your social network lively.

2. *Live videos*

You can have live videos on Instagram. These are a bit tricky as they have no room for editing. They literally stream live as you record them. However, they do provide a great opportunity to promote content.

Take event organizers for instance. They have an opening to further promote their event, hype it up to have people excited about it. They can have live videos of behind the scenes clips, showing the preparations, exclusive interviews and such.

Posting these on Instagram would make the viewers more interested in going to the event, as well as creating an interactive atmosphere for them.

The video doesn't have to be perfect. As long as the message is passed, then it has served its purpose. Furthermore, you are given the option of saving or discarding it once you finish making it. If you don't like how it sounds, you can always do away with it afterward.

Sharing live videos tends to create a bond with you and the viewers of the video. Of course, it will all depend on your creativity and relevance. Share something that is interesting, entertaining, or educative. Take advantage of this feature to improve your account stats.

3. Instagram Algorithm

The aim of Instagram is to have you on their app as long as possible. This explains the algorithms, which are essentially a way to have only relevant content appearing on your newsfeed.

Picture that boy trying to woo a girl; he would pay attention to her and notice the small details, then he would bring her favorite flowers to her or buy her the ice cream she loves most.

Similarly, Instagram finds out which posts a user

wants to see more and brings these to them. The relevance of this content is determined by a user's previous activity in the app, such as posts they have liked, commented on, and saved.

The feature is great for your business account as it gives you a greater chance to have your posts viewed despite the time they are posted.

You will need to present your posts in such a way that other users engage with them frequently; have the algorithm work to your advantage. This way, the posts will appear top of the newsfeeds of your followers to ensure that people are liking and commenting on more of your posts.

Have high-quality content that is relevant and engaging to attract their attention. Also post frequently so they don't forget about your account. Go to your Instagram Insights page to see how different posts perform and get to know which type of post to stick to.

There is a lot more you can do to increase the chances of users liking your content. Keep posted for more tips.

4. Instagram Collections

This is by far the very best addition yet to Instagram. Picture this: You are scrolling through images on the app, and you come across one of a restaurant that looks absolutely wonderful. You promise yourself that you will go there and then move on to other images.

Fast forward to a few weeks later when you want to go to that restaurant but cannot remember:

- Who posted it

- What it is called

- Where it is

There is no way of finding out other than scrolling through weeks' worth of images to find it.

The user who bumps into your page and later wants to show it to a friend, this is what they would have been forced to do before Instagram introduced the collections feature. It lets a user save posts to a collection. The user can also sort the saved posts and have different topics for different types of posts.

Encourage your followers to save your posts and share with friends later. You can get creative with this to ensure they remember this option and that way you won't lose potential clients to forgetfulness.

You will not be notified when a user saves your post to a collection. Saved videos or images are saved to a private tab that only the user can see and access.

Managing your Account

Photos you are tagged in

While creating your brand, there are things that you may want to be associated with and others not so much. Sometimes, however, it still happens that you are tagged in a photo that you would rather not have associated with your brand.

If you find yourself in such a situation, you may hide the photos or videos you are tagged in. Go to the photos you have been tagged in, click on the three dots at the top right corner, and change the options as desired.

You can have the photos you are tagged in appear on the 'photos of you' section automatically or choose manually which photos appear and which ones do not.

It is advisable to keep tabs on the photos you re tagged in, especially if you have the photos open for public viewing and not hidden.

Push Notifications

You can have the push notifications either on or off for different users that you follow. Turning on push notifications means that you will get notified each time they post something new.

To turn it on, go to the three dots that appear on the profile of a user and select 'Turn on push notifications.'

For your business account, you may not really be interested in being notified when another user posts something. However, you do want your audience to get such a notification.

Are you about to launch a new product? Have a promotion running, or an exciting deal where some of the items are going for a discounted price? Having people turn on the push notifications on Instagram would give you a platform to communicate with potential clients. When you post about it, users will be notified of it.

It reduces chances of missing the post, ensuring users actually see the post, and they may even share it with friends and family, further widening your reach. The push notifications feature increases your visibility and keeps you relevant in your circles.

Publishing Images and videos

Custom Stickers

This is another exciting feature on Instagram that brings it closer to Snapchat in terms of similarity. It is fairly new but interesting. If you like to take selfies, this feature should be interesting for you.

While uploading your story, you will see the new option to add a GIF. Tap on it to bring you all these cool moving stickers that you can add to your photo or video to make it more interesting.

There are also the hashtag stickers, another new addition on Instagram that takes hashtags to the next level. You can place a larger font of the hashtag on the image, to make it pop out more.

This is great for both personal accounts and business accounts. You can promote a hashtag more easily with this feature, by placing it in such a way that it is hard to miss.

The hashtag also enables you to appear on other people's explore pages, making you more visible to even more users. Become popular within your network by using this new feature.

You may promote your brand using this feature. Just have the slogan or logo as a hashtag and use this hard-to-miss hashtag which will stick in the memories of users. If it looks cool enough for the users, they may even take it up and use it in their posts which leads to free marketing for you.

Adding the hashtag sticker is also quite straightforward. Once you have chosen the image you wish to post, click on the hashtag in a white box and key in your desired tag, place it where you want and then proceed to post. There you have it, your hard-to-miss hashtag.

Multiple Photos Post

There was a time not so long ago when you could only post one image or video per post on Instagram; that time is long gone. Today, you can post multiple photos in a single post. So, when you take photos of products like similar bags in different colors, you can have them all in one post.

This feature saves you time and effort as well as

that of the viewer. They will only need to swipe left to see the images. You can have images with the same concept together for greater ease of navigation.

Click on the plus sign to begin with then tap on 'add multiple' on the bottom right. Choose the photos you want to post and then post them all at once.

Cover Thumbnail for Video

When you are posting videos on Instagram, you do it with the hope that it will have multiple views. You want to come back to a ridiculously high number of views. One thing that determines how many people watch your video is the video thumbnail.

The thumbnail tells a user what to expect from the video. Sometimes the very first second of your video may not really make a user feel the need to watch the video.

Maybe there is a specific shot that you are sure will create interest in the viewers. Instagram has got your back on this. You can change your cover shot and pick any frame from your video.

To change the cover shot, first, pick a video you would like to share. Go to the square icon and then use the bottom slider to pick the exact shot you would like to represent your video in. Pick one that is sure to have more people clicking to watch your video.

Multiple Instagram accounts

Yes, you can have multiple Instagram accounts. Have a business account and a personal account, or several business accounts, and switch between them easily with this feature.

You do not have to log out of one first and then log in to the other account; you can save loads of time now.

How? You might ask.

Follow these steps:

- Go to your profile.

- Click on the three dots at the top right corner. This should bring you to a menu with several options.

- Choose the 'add account' option.

- Follow the prompts to add your account successfully.

- Once your account is added, you can now switch between the accounts by clicking on the username on your profile. It is that fast and easy. You can have a maximum of 5 accounts. Open different accounts accordingly for your brand and manage them all easily.

Instagram keeps changing, and there are already prospects of more changes that will be made in the near future. To market your products successfully on Instagram, you will need to keep up with the changes.

There may be more opportunities to improve the impact your social media accounts have on your business, and you wouldn't want to miss out on them.

Link up your Instagram account with your other sites as well, such as Facebook, Twitter, and any websites if available. They will complement each other and can have collectively a larger audience than when they are separated.

There are many more features on Instagram apart from the ones mentioned here that serve to make the app what it is today. You can try out different things as you discover new ways of using the app for your benefit. Find what works for you and what does not.

How to Use Instagram for Marketing and to Earn Money

Instagram today has over 800 million users. Its popularity with the population internationally means that there are a large number of people using it at any given time. This makes it a great avenue for marketing.

Think about it; millions of users, all brought together by the social network, all potential clients for your business. What's better is that you can actually engage them in the app, and market your product or service to a large audience. You could reach unimaginable heights with your business on Instagram.

Did you know that you can also make money from Instagram?

You do not even have to be a professional marketer with papers to prove it. With a substantial following and the right moves, you could be on your way to making good money with Instagram marketing. Affiliate marketing needs some effort and knowledge of how to get the best out of it.

Whether you are a business owner or affiliate marketer, there is something for each of you here. Let's look at the strategies you should put in place as well as tips on how to improve your skill.

How to Make Money on Instagram

If you are a frequent user of Instagram, then you should think of monetizing your account. Earn some cash while doing what you like to do. Here are a few tips to have you on your way to making money.

Grow your following

The very first step you need to take to start making money on Instagram is to grow your following. It is a requirement of the trade, and the more you have the better for you.

Your following is what you sell to the people you want to pay you. They need to know that they can have a large audience to show their product to, and this is where you come in.

To increase your following, there are a few things you will need to ensure:

Have great quality content

This means the images and videos you post need to be of good quality. They should be relevant to the field you are interested in. For instance, if you are in the field of sports, then have sports-related content that is educative, entertaining, and visually attractive.

People tend to follow accounts with interesting posts, with the aim of seeing more of them so this should be your goal; to attract and keep people's interests.

Make use of shout-outs from other accounts

If you have used Instagram before, then you have seen people getting shout-outs from other users' accounts. That 'Follow my friend's account' message under a particular user's post is popular.

To get the most out of this, find a relevant user who has a good following. You may have friends or acquaintances that you can ask to give you a shout out and send some of their followers your way, especially on a post that is in your field.

Other than acquaintances, you can also find popular Instagram personalities that give shout outs frequently. Approach them to share your content and mention your username. People who view this content may take interest in your profile and visit it for more posts, possibly even following you to keep updated if they like it.

In case you have no acquaintances with a high following, you can always pay to get shout outs. To do this, you will need to identify a high-ranking influencer, preferably one who has very many followers and high engagement levels, preferably in your niche or at least closely related, for best results.

Next, you will approach the user to endorse your page by mentioning your username and asking his or her followers to check out your account.

Be Consistent

To gain more followers, while you ask for shout

outs and create good quality content, you need to be consistent with your posts. This means posting frequently and maintaining the quality of your posts throughout.

Posting once and then never going back for a month or two is no way to gain followers. On the contrary, they will 'un-follow' you if you do not show them what made them follow you in the first place.

Use Hashtags

Using relevant hashtags makes you more discoverable, giving more people a chance to follow you. Hashtags put you on the map. When users search for particular hashtags, they should be able to find your posts. This requires you to have well-tailored hashtags that are easy to find, and more likely to be searched for.

Find Brands to Partner with

Once you have a substantial following, you can now start looking for brands that will work with you. Remember the money needs to come from somewhere. These brands are what will pay to make use of your audience or your posts.

How many followers do you need? You might ask, well the more the merrier.

To start with, try to get at least 5000 followers. Already have more than 5000 followers? If your followers are in the hundreds of thousands or close to a million, then you probably do not need to find brands to partner with as they must have already approached you.

Where to look

You may have several brands in mind that you would like to partner with. You may approach them with your proposal and maybe they will agree to work with you. Keep in mind that larger brands may require a more influential Instagram user. But there are so many brands that would be willing to work with you.

If you have no idea where to start, we have great news for you. You can always join influencer networks. These tend to act as intermediaries and can link you up with potential brands. You as the influencer with a solid following will be connected with brands that need such influencers as yourself.

These platforms for you to network in include; Tribe, Buzzweb, and Influence.co, amongst others. They all offer different networking opportunities for you.

Some are good for you if you have a few thousand followers like Tribe. There you just look for brands to work with, create posts for the brand and submit them. If they approve it, you will get paid quickly.

For more than 5000 followers, try out Buzzweb where you can join many campaigns at once and get paid for all of them.

Depending on the network you join, you may get one that calculates potential monthly earnings for you depending on your followers. Other networks have brands that pay according to how much traffic your content drives, the people who like and comment or share.

Ways of earning Revenue

There are different paths you can take with earning money on Instagram. You can either earn directly or indirectly. Direct earning is from selling photos you post, or getting payments for tagging companies, posting their products or posts on their page for your audience to see.

The direct ways are simple where you get money for your audience's attention, or for photos that generated a lot of interaction on your profile. It is a quick way of earning money.

Indirect ways of earning from Instagram include driving traffic to the product of the specified brand, or a website, after which you get paid for the amount of traffic driven.

You can also earn from Instagram through affiliate marketing. With this, you can use the account to drive traffic to your website. Alternatively, you also have the option of using the account as a page to advertise on.

Therefore, you can post advertisements there for the audience to see, and any interested parties would come forward and ask for information on your comment section or through private messaging.

To drive traffic to a particular website, you can have a link to your account. Instagram allows a user to add a link to their bio section.

So, if you have a blog, for example, you can ask the viewers on your Instagram page to click on the link on your bio and get access to content on the site it links to.

Other than on your bio, you can add your link on posts, where you place it together with a caption. This is a great way to drive traffic to a website, and generally to advertise a brand and earn money for it.

Finally, you can have images that are relevant to different niches. There are hundreds of stock image sites where you can sell the images you have. Search for such sites on Google and you will find them. To get images that you can sell, you will need to be very creative.

You also need to look for popular niches to base your images on for a higher chance of having your images bought.

Tips to earn well on Instagram

Use hashtags effectively

Have followers relevant to your niche and what you are all about. Followers interested in what you have to show are more beneficial than followers who are only there to add to your followers' list.

Engage your audience. Ask for feedback and encourage commenting. More engagement levels lift you up in the eyes of potential partner brands, so you may end up earning more.

Try to keep your identity. You should try not to deviate from what your Instagram page is all about. As such, find brands that are close to your field to remain relevant for longer. This determines your image and affects future partnerships.

Buying Followers

You may have heard of the concept of buying followers. It is a quick way to increase your following. With the high demand for a large number of followers, there has been an increase in hacks to cheat your way out of acquiring followers the traditional way.

There are follower apps, generators, and other such hacks that can multiply your follower count. You may want to go to such lengths to make your account look more lucrative. But is it beneficial in the long run?

These followers that are bought or generated in such ways mentioned above are usually fake. The additional followers may not exist but are actually powered by bots. Now, this creates quite a problem for you in terms of engagement.

Fake accounts cannot engage with your posts. They can't like or comment on your post. The lack of engagement will have negative impacts on your account. If your analytics are not as good as expected, potential partners may choose to go with a different influencer, and you would lose chances to earn from your account.

Put in the work to get genuine followers, and improving your engagement levels, and you will be on the right path.

How to Use Instagram for Marketing

Instagram's popularity makes it a great platform for marketing. It has a large user base and its rates of engagement are quite high. This creates a great environment for marketing purposes.

Instagram can be quite complicated for a business owner. Where do you start? How do you start to engage your audience? And most importantly, how do you translate that into sales?

There are ways that you can use the app to market your business and grow your brand. We have put together strategies that you may use to connect with viewers and to ensure that you reach the target market through Instagram.

Maximize the use of hashtags

Hashtags happen to be a crucial factor for Instagram marketing success. They tend to put you on the map to people outside of your followers.

When a user searches for something that is within your field, you want them to be exposed to your posts.

General hashtags

These are easy to find. They are the ones a user is most likely to look for and are sure to drive users to your posts. You can have popular hashtags that have been used a lot like #family, #tbt which will drive a lot of traffic to your account.

While adding these, ensure they are related to

your posts, but general enough for easy finding.

Content hashtags

To get more targeted traffic, you can have hashtags that, although they are less frequently used, will attract people who want something specific. These are more content-specific and less popular.

They should describe what you offer, so one gets exactly what they wanted when they searched that hashtag. They are more likely to convert into sales.

Brand hashtags

You can also use hashtags to promote your brand by using your company name or a slogan that you associate with your brand. This will put you in the minds of other users.

If you get people to use the slogan, you can gain good marketing from other users, and make your brand stronger.

You can also use hashtags designed to bring more

followers specifically like #follow. These hashtags can be used together, you can have several hashtags in a single post, and they will all attract different users.

Since there is no limit on the number of hashtags to use, mix them up, using several of them to get more people seeing your page. However, be careful not to look too tacky or desperate by overdoing the hashtags.

Build and be involved in an Instagram Community

Every business owner knows the importance of good customer relationships, and that they are the key to the success of a business. Similarly, you need to nurture good relationships with Instagram users to keep them engaged.

To create a relationship with users, you can follow them, like and comment on their posts. They may feel the need to reciprocate and follow back. When users leave comments on your posts, reply to the comments to keep the conversation flowing.

Start conversations by asking questions or using humor. Make the users feel like they are your friend. An example would be posting an image with the question, "What are you having for breakfast this morning," as a way to spark conversation beyond you selling your product or service.

Post more about what your company has been up to. If you had an event, post photos of the event, maybe even have some employees' photos on there to make the account more human.

If users feel they can relate to you, they may be more skewed towards using your brand and telling people about it. Make them feel like they are part of the community.

Use Sponsored Ads

Sponsored Ads are those posts that appear in your newsfeed advertising something. Such posts are very advantageous for you so they can be shown to users who are not following you.

As long as the user fits your target audience, you can show your ad on their newsfeed.

More and more businesses are using sponsored ads to get a larger reach for their marketing campaigns. You will be required to part with some of your cash to have a sponsored ad, but you can set an ad budget to keep from using too much money.

Have interesting content that is tailored to the target audience depending on their demographics. If there is a specific post that did extremely well in terms of user engagement, why not use it on your sponsored ad?

Depending on the audience, you can have different content for the sponsored ads, all running at the same time. This will cater to more people. You can also have photos, videos, Instagram stories, or carousel on your sponsored ad, as you please.

Keep Track of your Metrics

The performance of your Instagram determines

your next steps. It also tells you how successful different moves are and where there is room for improvement. The metrics that you need to keep track of include:

Follower Growth

You need to keep adding followers. If your followers are not increasing then that might point to a problem. The total number of followers may not be as important as how many new followers you have gotten over a specific period of time. Having low follower growth rate tells you to change your strategy to increase followers, so keep track of this.

Engagement rate

Are users engaging with you? Are the likes and comments increasing or not? You should be more precise by looking at the level of engagement brought by different posts. You may get a pattern and find posts that people seem to favor over others and have more similar content to post.

Click through rate of URLs

You can tell how many people are clicking on the link on your bio. If the number is extremely low, then it might be time to change your tactics and find better ways to bring traffic to click on that link.

Such metrics keep you on your toes. You get to know which strategies are working and which are not. You also understand your audience and what they like, all of which are required to be more effective on Instagram.

Partner with Influencers

Sometimes you may need a bit of help with getting your brand out there. One strategy that is sure to work is working with influencers in your industry.

These are people with a large following of users who trust recommendations they make. The influencers tend to have a wide reach as well as the trust of the people. This is important for a new brand that is just starting out as people may not trust it.

The influencers will help get your brand to users, they may give a shout out on their accounts or post your products for their followers to see, maybe even promote an event or contest that you plan to hold.

You will need to choose an influencer who is relevant in your field, so as to generate traffic that is more targeted.

Also, think of a more long-term step with the influencer compared to short-term efforts. You can make use of the attention from their audience to launch several campaigns over a period of time.

Create more awareness for your brand like this.

Hold Contests

People love competitions. You can hold contests and have giveaways to increase engagement and have people talking about your brand. These require your creativity. It needs to be something interesting that people will actually want to do.

The most popular contest on Instagram is the image contest that can be presented in different ways. For instance, having them share a specific image on their account with a hashtag generated by you. The one with the most likes on that image wins the contest.

Such contests are good as they help you have more viewers seeing your brand and possibly more followers.

Consider User-submitted photos

Collection of user-submitted photos is a great way to kill two birds with one stone. Increase user-generation and get content to post on your account while you are at it.

You can get the people to submit photos by holding a contest of some sort, where the most creative gets featured on your account. In return, you can offer to tag them in the post.

Of course, while choosing the photos to post,

ensure that they are most beneficial to you.

The photos should:

- Fit with your brand

- Be from a user with a substantial following

- Be appropriate

- Be relevant to your field

Be consistent in your posts

You will need to post frequently to remain relevant. However, refrain from posting too frequently. If all your followers see are posts from your account, they will un-follow you to keep from seeing too many of your posts.

If you find problems posting, you can always opt for the pre-scheduled posts which you choose in advance and have them posted at the designated times each day without you having to post them every other day.

Instagram marketing is best done with a business

account, as it has more tools and gives you more insights. There is no specific method to have a sure win with Instagram marketing.

You can, however, use the tips given to improve results. Just try out different techniques, finding which works best for your business using the strategies mentioned to guide you. Use Instagram marketing, together with other social media marketing, to grow your brand and increase sales or get into affiliate marketing to earn from your Instagram account.

Chapter 2 : Email Marketing

Email marketing refers to the process of sending a commercial message, basically to a group of people via email. If you look at email marketing in a wider view, each mail you send to a prospective or current customer is regarded as email marketing. Additionally, it involves using email to send advertisements, ask for business, solicit for sales or donations, and the aim is to build trust, loyalty, and awareness of one's brand.

Email marketing has undergone growth over the years. The first mass email sent out was in 1978, by **Gary Thuerk**, of Digital Equipment Corporation. It was sent to about 400 potential customers. This mass email resulted in sales worth thirteen million for this company and emphasized the impact of marketing via emails. However, as email marketing developed, users started blocking content from emails with filters and blocking programs.

So as to effectively relay message via email, marketers came up with a way of pushing the content through to the end user without being cut off by automatic filters and spam removing software. Consequently, this led to the birth of triggered marketing emails which are sent out to specific users based on their tracked patterns of online browsing. In the earlier years, it was difficult to measure the effectiveness of marketing campaigns because target markets could not be properly defined. Email marketing is beneficial as it allows marketers to point out returns on investments as well as measure and improve efficiency.

Moreover, email marketing allows marketers to see response from users in real time, and to monitor the progress and effectiveness of their campaign in market penetration.

Marketing via emails can be done in different ways:

- *Transactional emails*

Such emails are usually triggered based on a customer's action with an entity. For an email to be regarded as a transactional or relationship message, the primary purpose of the communication should be to facilitate, complete, or confirm a commercial transaction that the recipient has previously agreed to enter into with the sender along with a few other narrow definitions of transactional messaging. Triggered transactional messages include dropped basket messages, password reset emails, purchase or order confirmation emails, order status emails, recorder emails, as well as email receipts.

The basic aim of a transactional email is to relay information about the action that triggered it. However, because of the high open rates, transactional emails provide a chance to introduce, or extend the email relationship with customers or subscribers, to anticipate and answer questions, or to cross-sell or up-sell products and services.

Several email newsletter software vendors also

offer transactional email support offering companies the platform to include promotional messages within the body of transactional emails. Software vendors also exist that offer specialized transactional email marketing services which include providing targeted and personalized transactional email messages and running specific marketing campaigns.

- *Direct emails*

This involves sending an email with the single aim of relaying a promotional message; for instance, a special offer or product catalog. Organizations usually collect a list of customer or prospect email addresses to send direct promotional messages to, or they rent a list of email addresses from service companies.

- *Mobile email marketing*

Email marketing currently develops large amounts of traffic via smartphones and tablets. Marketers are researching ways of capturing the attention of users in span and volume. The problem is that the rate of delivery is still low because of the strong filters, and several users have multiple email accounts for different functions. Since emails are generated as per the tracked behavior of customers, it is not impossible to tailor promotional material to their requirements and to present relevant details to potential buyers. Due to this, modern email marketing is regarded as a pull strategy rather than a push strategy.

Email marketing vs Traditional mail

There are pros and cons when using email marketing as opposed to traditional advertising mail.

Pros

Email marketing is useful for companies because:

- An accurate tracking of a return on investment can be done. Email marketing is always reported second only to search marketing when it comes to effective online marketing options.

- Secondly, it is cheaper and faster compared to traditional mail due to its cost as well as the time needed in a traditional mail campaign for producing artwork, printing, addressing, and mailing.

- Additionally, entities that send out bulks of emails can use an email service provider to collect information about the recipients' behavior. The insights provided by consumer response to email marketing assists businesses and organizations to understand and utilize behavior of consumers.

- Emails also provide a cost-effective method to test different marketing content such as visual, creative, marketing copy, as well as multimedia assets. Furthermore, the data collected by testing in the email channel can be used across all channels of marketing campaigns in both print and digital.

- Advertisers can also reach a good number of email subscribers who have opted in.

- Compared to standard email, direct email marketing produces a higher rate of response as well as a higher average order value for e-commerce businesses.

Cons

Deliverability of emails is an issue and companies should make sure that their program does not violate spam laws.

Opt-in email marketing

This is also known as permission marketing. It is a method of email advertising where the recipient has consented to receive it. This is one of the methods developed by marketers to get rid of the deliverability issue. This method is intended to bring a high degree of satisfaction between a consumer and a marketer. By using opt-in email advertising, the email will be anticipated by a consumer. It will be assumed that the consumer wants to receive it and they will be more personal and relevant to the consumers compared to untargeted adverts.

An example of this is a newsletter sent to an advertising company's customers. They notify customers of upcoming events, promotions, as well as new products.

A beginner's guide to successful email marketing

Step one: Being permitted

There is no email campaign that can be set up without getting permission. So, the first step is to focus on building a sizeable email list. You can do this in several ways; you may decide to offer something for free, or simply give out newsletters or product samples. It is however important for you to have a clear aim when asking for an address. Some factors to consider are:

- How do I gain by giving you my email address?

- Will you spam me?

- How often will you email me?

- Are there discounts?

- Will you send me more junk or relevant offers?

Even though a majority of all reputable email service providers strive to prevent your emails from being blocked by major internet service providers, they have no control where your email will land, whether inbox or spam box. Most of them will help you by providing you with a quality score, but getting whitelisted is the best way of ensuring that your emails will get a proper delivery. Whitelisting is like being marked as a friend and the best way of achieving this is by being added to a recipient's address book. You do this by giving instructions to do so at the top of each email, especially on the initial thank you and first follow-up email.

Step two: Play the game of numbers

Email marketing is all about expectations, and it's your job to set them. If your call to action is powerful, and your follow-up is consistent, then you can expect a positive campaign. If you plan to send an email per week but send them daily, you are headed for failure. On the other hand, if someone expects daily updates, and you don't send, they will obviously get upset.

This is the reason why the initial follow-up is quite important to the success of your email marketing. A majority of email service providers offer you the option of creating an autoresponder sequence, and you should take advantage of it. The first follow-up should be sent immediately as a way of introducing yourself and detailing what you plan on doing with your new subscriber's email address.

You need to ask yourself whether your messaging is consistent with your set expectations.

Newsletters

Do you know the difference between a good and bad newsletter? You will know you have received a bad newsletter if you do not remember asking to receive it. Basically this happens when a business is unable to maintain a regular email routine or uses a poor form and manually adds you to their list after receiving a business card or personal email. On the other hand, the most compelling ones are those that do a great job of blending messages and updates. For example, the email contains a list of products and images, but is balanced by a personal message or a friendly update.

The basic rule is to always use your newsletter as a way of furthering your relationship with the reader or customer rather than pitching them. Use the pitch for unique updates, offers, and announcements.

As a marketer, one of the hurdles I bump into most of the time is that I neglect my list until when I have something to sell. This is not wise at all. This is where an autoresponder comes in and it is recommended that you schedule content to be delivered on a regular basis over several months. The advantage of this is that when you need to announce a new product or sale, you can rely on the fact that you have already been in touch, and built a relationship over time. Please ensure that you schedule your autoresponder on specific days so that you know when you can afford to send an email.

Just in case you find yourself questioning whether a certain email is one too many, then it probably is.

Step three: Segmentation and Analysis

The three most important ones are open rate, click through rate, and unsubscribes. The open rate will inform you of how well you have built your relationship; if the number is low, it means that people have started deleting upon receipt. This means you need to work harder on offering value and managing expectations.

Secondly, if your CTR is low it means that your message is not well targeted or simply not going through. You need to concentrate on improving your copy.

Lastly, if the un-subscription rate is high compared to your opt-in rate, then you are past the point of building value and writing good copies. There is some serious work to be done here. Try to analyze why people are leaving and act on the leaks. In case they are leaving due to a certain auto-responder email, then work on it. If they leave after marketing messages, work on the way your offers are presented. In case they are leaving early in your funnel, you need to fix the original call to action so that it's in sync with what you are sending out.

Email analytics are vital as they will give you specific clues as to what you're not doing right.

Segmentation

This is the practice of splitting up your email list into groups that are more targeted. When you divide your list this way, you will have the ability to send communication that is more targeted. Selected customers need both product and sales updates, while another section only wants to hear about new releases. If you don't give them a chance to choose, you will risk losing them. With segmentation, you can broadcast only to those that didn't open your last message (ask why) or to those that showed interest. Furthermore, you can also split test messaging amongst groups so as to refine your best practices.

Reasons for using email marketing

This is a solution that is cost effective and gives you the power to reach your customers via their inbox. Lots of facts exist to support email marketing benefits:

- Almost ninety percent of adults in the US prefer receiving promotional emails from companies they conduct business with.

- Also, email is almost forty times more

effective than Facebook and Twitter combined when it comes to helping your business acquire new customers.

- Building credibility.

People will always do business with people they know, like, and trust. Email gives you the ability to build credibility with your audience by sharing helpful as well as informative content.

- Call generation

When done in the correct way, email marketing will enable you to reach the right person, with the right offer and at the right time.

- Improved donations

As efforts of fundraising move online, nonprofits need to change their outreach efforts too.

- Strengthening relationships

In case you need to build strong relationships with customers, it's important to have an effective tool for communicating with the people who matter most to you in business. Email offers you the ability to stay at the top of your mind and keep you engaged in your business during your busy season and the sluggish times of the year.

- Boost communication

In case your business relies on having a reliable way to communicate with your members and clients, you need to have a communication channel you can trust.

- Build your brand

With emails, you have the ability to strengthen brand recognition with new and potential clients, and extend your coverage when people forward or share your message with a friend.

- Boost sales

When you have an audience of people who are interested in receiving updates from your business, you will be able to reason differently about how you boost sales all year round.

- Email marketing will also give you the metrics you require to see how your emails are performing. The insights will help you market smarter, as well as give you the advantage of better understanding the needs and interests of your customer base.

- You will also get started quite fast. With marketing software such as Constant Contact, you will have the tools and training you need to get started quickly. It does not matter the level of marketing experience you have or expertise.

- Additionally, you can reach people on any device.

- With an email marketing provider, you have access to professionally-designed email templates. These templates are designed in such a way that it is quicker and easier to get your message to your audience and make sure that you look professional.

- It will also help in increasing web traffic.

How to build an email list

A healthy email list is one of the best marketing assets of a small business. Even though proper management and use of your email file will greatly generate revenue, the main challenge is always to create the email list itself. Inbox clutter is rising and customers are becoming more sensitive towards any communication that is not desired; marketers need to develop their lists of subscribers with a lot of care and relevance.

Luckily, there are several easy but effective methods of creating an email list; traditional online and offline tactics, paid search, direct mail, events, as well as special offers. The factors to consider when creating an email list are:

- Using the tactics responsibly

- Abiding by all the legal requirements

- Respecting the preferences of subscribers

Direct mail

Advertise email sign-up in all catalogs, directory ads, as well as direct-mail order forms. A simple checkbox accompanied by a field for writing in an email address on bills, rebate cards, and renewal of subscriptions is all you need to give to make your list grow. When you use this method, ensure that you email all new subscribers as soon as you can. Chances will be that much time has elapsed since they mailed the form, and it's advisable to keep your brand fresh in their minds and go on with the dialogue.

Email sign-up boxes

When you place a clear and conspicuous form on your website, you will be able to facilitate email sign-ups for your website visitors. This form of acquisition is not only effective but quite simple to implement. Also, there are a few important things one should keep in mind when using this tactic:

- Maintain the appearance and feel of all website sign-up boxes clean and consistent as this will make them more reputable, easy to find, and familiar to your audience.

- Secondly, try to place sign-up boxes either as part of the top banner or immediately below. A majority of test results have shown that the ones located near the top of the website perform better compared to those found at the footer area.

- Additionally, couple your sign-up boxes with a clear description of what they have to gain. Inform your customers of exactly what they should expect when signing up, and market the benefits of being on the email list. This can be as simple as promoting the general pros of the channel such as being able to receive information and offers faster, and that it's also eco-friendly.

Account registration and online e-commerce forms

Registration of sites is the most common as well as effective way of acquisition of marketers. A research revealed that seventy percent of marketers regard site registration effective when it comes to both quality and quantity. So, you need to make sure to incorporate email sign-up into all account registration and e-commerce forms on your website. For one to effectively do this, follow these:

- The incentive for registration is clear and relevant to your targeted audience

- The benefits of registration for your email program are listed clearly

- Geographic as well as demographic information is collected for segmentation

- The call to action is prominently displayed

Word of mouth

For subscribers who have been on your list for a long time, a small discount, or incentive, will make them spread the word. Marketers need to take advantage of word-of-mouth marketing by incorporating email sign-up on viral components such as features that allow site visitors to forward products, services, wish lists, online information, and other notifications to their friends.

This tactic is effective for new sign-ups and sweepstake entries because such subscribers are always eager to spread the word to family and friends. Take advantage of enthusiasm and utilize the timing by providing an opportunity for referral immediately after a user has opted in.

It's advisable to ask the referrer not only for a friend's email address, but also for a name so that the message can be personalized. Moreover, do not forget to add the referee's full name to the email as well. When you reference whom the email was recommended by, you will have instant credibility and your conversion rates will skyrocket.

Customer requests and downloads

When those who visit your website ask for online price quotes, catalogs, or company information, make sure to ask for their email addresses. This list-growth practice is mostly effective for business-to-business marketers, catalogers and other businesses that may lack e-commerce websites. You need to save any new documentation as a PDF for download and require that individuals enter their names and email addresses for them to access it.

The value of information that you offer is directly proportional to the amount of personal data your customers are willing to provide, so as to make a fair trade-off. A highly anticipated white paper or report can garner a high number of new email subscribers who are openly expressing interest in your brand, so don't waste this opportunity.

Point of sale

For retail stores, asking customers for their email addresses at the POS is a proven method. To put this method into action, it is important for your associates to:

- Request customers for their email addresses

- Explain to your customers the benefits of your email program

- Let your customers know exactly what to expect in terms of email frequency and content

- Read through the email address to verify correct spelling and minimize the risk of error

Lastly, training of employees and in-store signage promotion of your program can adequately support this effort.

Send a welcome email offering a free gift with any purchase

For you to encourage your customers to give out their email addresses, think about offering a free product with their next buy. An email can be sent to confirm the email address and you can include a free offer coupon. This will validate the email address and will encourage the customers to shop once more.

Call-center representatives

You need to know that customers are highly receptive when on customer service calls. You will have their full attention and you need to use it to your advantage by requesting email addresses. You will be shocked at how many of them will comply. Furthermore, if your customer representatives are writing their own emails to follow up with customers, make sure that they put a link to an email sign-up form in their email signatures.

Legal requirements for email marketing in selected countries

Australia

The Australian Spam Act 2003 is enforced by the Australian Communications and Media Authority. The act defines the terms of unsolicited electronic messages, how unsubscribe functions must work for commercial messages, and other key information.

Canada

The Canada anti-spam law was effected in July 1, 2014. It requires an explicit or implicit opt-in from users, and the maximum fines for non-compliance are one million dollars for individuals and ten for businesses.

European Union

In the year 2002, the European Union introduced the Directive on Privacy and Electronic Communications. Article 13 of the directive prohibits the use of personal email addresses for purposes of marketing. This directive establishes the opt-in regime, where emails that are unsolicited may be sent only with prior agreement of the recipient; however, this does not apply to business email addresses.

United States

The CAN-SPAM Act of 2003 was passed by Congress as a direct response because of the growing number of complaints about spam emails. Congress directed that those who send commercial emails should not mislead recipients over the source or content, and that all those who receive them have a right to decline them. Furthermore, the act authorizes a 16,000 dollar penalty per violation for spamming each individual recipient.

However, this act does not ban spam emailing outright, but imposes laws on using deceptive methods of marketing through false or misleading headlines. Additionally, there are conditions which email marketers have to meet in terms of their format, content, and labeling. To show compliance with the Act's regulation of commercial email, services also need users to authenticate their return address and include a valid physical address, provide a one-click unsubscribe feature, and prohibit importing lists of purchased addresses that may not have given valid permission.

Quick tips for email marketing in small businesses

- Avoid experimenting with the sender field

A name that can be easily recognized in the sender field is a very good thing. Your sender field needs to be consistent and make it simple for whoever reads it to see who sent it. This is because this is the first thing that readers look at when deciding whether to open an email or not.

- Have a killer subject line

The second thing is to sway the reader's attention to your subject line. Try to be enticing, appeal to your readers' fears, needs, likes, and ambitions. Additionally, be short and snappy.

- Talk to your reader

Whether your email is being sent to 5 people or 5,000, write for an audience of one. Build a mental image of your model reader. Be vivid and talk to them directly, just as you would if you were talking to them in person.

- Be personal

If you know the name of your reader, use Constant Contact's email marketing software to automatically include it in your emails. You can also use it in the main message of your email to keep the reader engaged. But don't overdo it. Jamming your reader's name into every sentence may sound a bit creepy. The aim is to sound natural.

- Offer value

Chances are that your reader doesn't care about that new member of staff you are so keen to announce. What they do want is the answer to a problem. Ultimately, that's what every reader wants. When you provide value, your emails get read.

- Make it snappy

The average person's inbox is something of a battlefield. They want to keep the number of unread emails under control, which isn't easy when they receive dozens of emails daily. Now, your reader has given you permission to be in their inbox. Honor that by respecting their time and keeping your content snappy. If it takes longer than a minute or two to absorb the message, it might be time for a rethink.

- Make the links and call to action obvious

You want your reader to click through to an article? Then make sure the buttons or hyperlinks stand out, and put your main call to action near the top. Don't expect your reader to do the guesswork.

- Segment your list of subscribers

The more targeted your message, the better you can expect your results to be. That means you need to gather as much information and insight about your subscribers as possible. Let's say you run a high street fashion store and are offering a half-price weekend in one of your branches. You want your subscribers who live near that branch to know about the offer, but it's a pretty useless message for anyone that doesn't live near the store in question. List segmentation lets you target the people that matter, with a message that matters.

- Ensure that your email is mobile optimized

Around two-thirds of email is opened on a smartphone or tablet. If your email design doesn't look great and function flawlessly on mobile devices, you could be alienating more than 60% of your audience.

- Test without tiring

Do your links go to the right page? Does the design look as it should in all of the most popular email clients? Do your images match your content? Run multiple tests – and send multiple test emails – before you go for the big launch.

- Split test

Sometimes the slightest tweak to a send title, layout, body copy message, or call to action can make a big difference to the effectiveness of your campaign. Split-testing is when you send slightly different versions of the same email to a sample of your subscribers. In Constant Contact it's simple to compare the results, and then you can send the best performing version to the rest of your subscribers. It's an easy way to squeeze every last drop from your campaign.

Email marketing doesn't need to be tricky, and it remains one of the best possible marketing techniques for reaching out to your audience.

Email marketing is an area all businesses should invest time and energy in. Even the smallest of businesses needs to be focused on growing their email list from the moment the website goes live. Your subscribers are your leads; they are your past and potential customers.

Email marketing gives you the opportunity to sell, educate, build brand awareness, and loyalty. It's possible to create multiple lists of subscribers for targeted marketing opportunities.

Chapter 3 : Twitter Marketing

Twitter was launched in 2006. It has since grown into one of the most popular social media platforms for brands, organizations, and individuals. It allows users to share real-time short messages with their followers.

Despite its massive audience, some still ask, "What is Twitter?" What is the need for sharing tweets online? Why would you want to attract more followers on Twitter? Is it just about posting short messages and attracting many followers?

With a large number of people using Twitter every day, it is evident that there is something much more that it offers the users. If you do not have the slightest idea of what Twitter is and how to use it, well, stick with us and learn what it is and how you can use it for marketing and even more.

So, what is Twitter?

Twitter is an Android app. From the name, it is an app that allows people to communicate in real-time short messages called tweets. Its real-time nature makes it different from other social media platforms.

Twitter is a form of texting that allows you to broadcast the text, blogs, and instant messages with brief content all over the site. It works like a micro-blogging site with the posts limited to slightly over 140 characters

Twitter has become a phenomenon with more than 313 million monthly active users. It has transformed the manner people consume content. Many people turn to Twitter for the latest news and updates.

This makes the platform a prime market for various products and services. It is, therefore, a great tool to add to your online marketing strategies to reach a wider audience and to create more visibility for your products or services.

The main Twitter Features

There are tools that make it possible to connect with other Twitter users. We are going to look at the three main tools and how you can use them.

1. Mentions

Mentions allow you to directly tag your followers in your tweets. This way, you can grab their attention and make your tweet stand out from the other tweets in their feeds.

You can tag anyone or any business. You only have to be nice and courteous by ensuring that you mention them in what will interest them.

2. Hashtags

This tool allows users to start and contribute to a group conversation on the site. You can click on the hashtag on a post to see people who are participating in the conversation. This will help you to keep track of the conversation.

As a brand, you can use a hashtag such as

#keepfit to promote your fitness business.

3. Live videos

Twitter has been on the live streaming wave for a long time. You can use the periscope to host question and answer sessions, events, and live conversations with your followers.

Periscope streams will appear in your followers' feeds. They stand out more than the normal texts and images, making them great tools for your online campaign.

Create a Twitter account today and implement it for your online business growth. Use these features and others to reach your target audience.

How Twitter Works: The different functionalities

Twitter has different functionalities that make it what it is. We will be going through these functionalities and shedding more light on the features mentioned in the first chapter.

Before we look at those, let us look at some of the terms associated with Twitter. Here are some of them and their meanings:

- **Tweets-** These are the actual posts that you make on your feed. As a brand, you can scan through other users' tweets to determine what interests them the most. This will enable you to produce high-value target-based content.

- **Home/feed-** This refers to a chronological collection of tweets made by the twitter users.

- **Notifications-** This is a list of all activities related to your profile such as mentions, retweets, likes, new followers, suggestion or additions to public lists and new tweets.

This feature makes it possible to keep records of your followers as well as acknowledging them and producing relevant content that will excite them.

- **_Messages_**- Direct messaging allows private conversations between you and your followers who want to make private inquiries.

- **_Following_**- This is a list of users you follow on the platform. You can follow influential brands and people in your industry for the opportunity to learn more from them.

They may follow you back, thus creating more audience for your business.

- **_Followers_**- This refers to the list of Twitter users who follow you. Despite the fact that your posts are public, they will appear in the feeds of your followers, thus, grabbing their attention.

Followers are like your customers and prospects. If they like your content, they will participate and retweet the content to evangelize your brand.

- **Likes**- Simply click the small heart icon to like a tweet. It is a great way to acknowledge and appreciate other users' messages.

You can also use it as a tool to attract more followers. People will notice you when you constantly like their posts and they may spare some time to learn more about your brand.

- **Retweets**- This is re-sharing an original tweet by clicking the small circle icon on the tweet. It acts as a way of endorsing the idea or message of other users.

Your retweets will forever be associated with your brand; make sure that whatever you retweet will not impact negatively on your brand.

The different functionalities of Twitter

1. *Customized Tweet Alert*

You may be dealing with many tweets, which

makes it easy to miss out on important tweets from other brands or people. For this reason, you need to customize your Twitter account to send you an SMS notification of new tweets. This way, you will not miss out on an important tweet.

Simply log onto your account, click on the user profile you want to follow, and click the "following" button. Select the "Turn on mobile notifications" and click on the "Set up phone" Make sure that your mobile device is supported by Twitter.

2. *Create Twitter Moments*

This feature was previously available to specific organizations and influencers. Today, anyone can use the feature to create moments on the web or mobile app.

Twitter moments give you an instant record of every Twitter activity that interests you. It saves time and keeps you updated.

It is also possible to create a story for your brand

using moments and easily share it as a curated post. To create moments, log into your Twitter account. Click on the moment's tab and then select "Create new moment."

Tap on the "Set cover" to upload an image from your computer or from the tweet. Go through the moment to ensure that everything is in place before you finally click the "publish" icon.

3. Keyboard shortcuts

Every second is important in business. You should find ways to optimize the time you spend on Twitter. Twitter has keyboard shortcuts for easy and quick account navigations.

4. Advanced search

You can use the advanced search to stay ahead of your competitors if you are familiar with the search terms. Simply type the keyword in the search window, click the "more options" icon and select the "Advanced search" option. Fill in the fields and finally click the "search" button.

Twitter is an important marketing venue which you should fully exploit to grow your business by reaching to your prospects and other leaders in your industry.

5. *Pin a tweet permanently*

Twitter is a great online marketing tool for small and big businesses. Having a perfect Twitter profile is essential for the success of your online visibility.

You can pin one tweet. Simply log into your account and choose the post you want to pin on your profile.

Attach up to 4 images in a tweet

The consumption of text document is constantly diminishing. Add images to your tweet to increase traffic on your page. Make the image consistent with your message.

Twitter allows you to add up to 4 images in a single tweet. More importantly, you are allowed to tag up to 10 people in every image.

6. *Go live with Periscope*

Live videos have become popular in recent years and Twitter has been on the live streaming wave for a long time.

Use Periscope to host question and answer sessions, and live conversations with your follower. Periscope streams will appear in your followers' feeds and they will stand out more than the normal texts and images.

Add a Periscope hashtag to your page and host it when most of your audience is online. Make each session entertaining to increase engagement with your followers.

For your Twitter marketing campaign to be a success, you need to put in some effort and be as creative and dynamic as possible. There is no one single fit-all tweet for all business niches.

It is recommended that you do your own research to effectively utilize these features for brand, products, or services marketing. Familiarise yourself with the features and find other creative ways you can use to increase your visibility and conversions.

How to Use Twitter for Marketing and to Earn Money

There are over 300 million active monthly Twitter users. Most of these users are the youth, which makes this platform a great avenue for online promotions. The hundreds of millions of active users also provides a potential market for brands to showcase their products and to convert the followers into leads.

Starting up a Twitter account for your brand is not an uphill task. Anyone can create a Twitter profile, upload their profile image, fill out the bio-field, and post their first tweet.

What needs more of your attention is how to grow your Twitter page and turn it into a traffic conversion tool. After all, converting traffic should be your main objective of the Twitter marketing campaign.

There is more to gaining a real and loyal following on Twitter than simply sending out tweets whenever you feel like. You need to get the attention of your followers, engage and interact with them to unlock new opportunities for the growth of your brand.

What makes Twitter different?

Your approach to your Twitter marketing campaign should be different from the approach you use on other social media platforms such as Facebook. You need to understand how Twitter works and its position in the social media landscape.

Some of the main ways you can use this platform include:

- Sharing messages and posts

- To interact with your customers

- Building your brand

- Network with other brands in the industry

- Managing your brand reputation

- Showcasing your products and interacting with your followers

It is, therefore, evident that Twitter activities are audience-based. You should provide your audience with high-quality content to get their attention and loyalty.

If you are interested in more than just setting up your profile and following the influencers, keep reading. You will learn how to promote your brand on Twitter like a pro.

Twitter Marketing Strategies

1. *Participate in Twitter Chats*

A question like, "How do I get more followers on my Twitter handle?" is common amongst many brands. But on your journey to becoming a pro with a Twitter campaign, your main concern should be, "How do you get more active followers?"

Twitter chats are the answer to your question. Twitter chats enable you to gain exposure in your industry, grow your following, and have a better interaction with your readers.

Interacting with the right audience will encourage them to give feedback to your tweets, share your tweets, and amplify your message.

You need to add value to the chats and make your tweets different from the rest. For instance, creating a special graphic will be more appealing than normal tweets.

Replying to chats will earn you real followers. The majority of your tweets should be replies to your audience. Remember to @mention them so that they are notified about the reply in their feeds.

Make follow-ups by replying, retweeting, and liking your followers' tweets to keep your relationship with them alive.

2. *Plan Ahead*

Launch your campaigns at least two to three weeks before the actual time. By late November, you should have tweets and content ready for the Christmas holidays.

Planning ahead will give you enough time to generate high-quality content that will perfectly fit the trending hashtags and topics. On the special day, follow any trending hashtags and do some real-time marketing for your brand.

Run timely Twitter promotions. Plan ahead and start the campaign at the right time to increase your success rate. Properly timed tweets will ensure that the promotions reach the audience at the right time and increase the conversion rate.

3. Make Your Tweets Conversational

It is a pity that many brand tweets do not encourage any conversation. Make your brand different by giving room for conversation and engagement.

Below is how you can increase interaction with

your audience:

- Tweet out questions as often as possible.

- Make at least 30% of your tweets replies to other people.

- Add a line of your own insights to your Twitter link to spark a conversation with your followers.

- Customize your post to tweet directly to your audience. Instead of a blog post title or link, you can tweet something more engaging like, "What is your view about this new post?"

A highly conversational tweet will lead to additional activities on your Twitter page, resulting from the higher engagement. Replies could also give you more followers and prompt them to buy your products.

4. Set goals and milestones

Determine the purpose and objectives of your

tweets. Your goal may be to gain more followers, increase awareness about your products, or to increase sales. Attach or link the goals to your reasons and continuously measure the achievements of your promotion. Your marketing strategy will be incomplete without a defined objective that you intend to accomplish by the end of the campaign.

Without goals, objectives, and milestones, you are bound to make mistakes and you will not even realize the mistakes early enough to make corrections.

Some brands simply publish content and then pray for miracles to improve their brand standing. But how possible are such miracles?

All your goals should be time-based; it could be monthly, weekly, or annually depending on your business niche. This will enable you to evaluate your performance within the specified period and make necessary adjustments for better future performance.

Use tools like Sprout Social or Google Analytics to track your activities and achievements. Make sure that your goals are achievable and realistic.

5. *Twitter video*

Live videos have become popular in recent years. Twitter has been on the live streaming wave for a long time.

Use the periscope to host question and answer sessions, events, and live conversations with your followers. Periscope streams will appear in your followers' feeds. They stand out more than the normal texts and images.

Add a periscope hashtag to your page and hold live sessions when most of your audience is online. Make each session entertaining to attract a bigger audience.

You can also opt for Twitter's native video feature, which allows you to record 140-second videos and upload them directly to your Twitter page.

6. *Viralpost*

The viralpost feature is a great and quick way to handle your Twitter promotion. The chances that your audience will see the posts are higher.

Viralpost increases engagement on your account which may result in more lead generation for your business.

7. *Run seasonal and trendy promotions*

Launch different promotions for different seasons. Always be relevant, flexible, and trendy. Understand the seasons and what interests your followers each season.

You also need to keep your ears to the ground for what is trending. This way, you will be able to create content that is always interesting and relevant.

8. *Partner with a co-promoter*

Partner with other brands on Twitter to get more exposure and to increase social connections for your business. You can also host a joint Twitter Chat with other influencers.

Quick Tips

Below are some things you can use Twitter and your following for to grow your business:

- Crowdsource to bring in contributions from your followers to fund a business idea.

- Selling your products should be the core objective of your Twitter campaign. Give your audience a clear call to action.

You can take it a notch higher by giving discounted products to encourage more traffic and conversion.

- Produce your own Twitter-related services. Make sure to study your audience and create a Twitter-related product/service that will be useful to them.

Something like an automatic mention generation will really excite the audience.

- Use promoted tweets because:

  1. Twitter is not so crowded with ads like Google or other online marketing sites. This makes Promoted tweets cheaper than the other ads.

  2. Promoted tweets enable you to reach a larger audience, thus more traffic to your website. This in turn leads to a higher lead generation for your business.

You have the option to choose your preferred target audience. This makes it easy to customize ads and the landing page to meet their specific needs.

  3. Promoted tweets are mobile friendly, making them great since many people use mobile devices to tweet.

  4. Promoted tweets increase your chances

of interacting with customers. It is possible for followers to like your tweets, leave comments, or retweet.

Treat each comment as an opportunity to strike a conversation with customers.

- Hold a Twitter contest to get more engagements and followers to your account.

- Discover new leads based on their bios and tweets. You can search a particular audience segment, say, skaters, using the search engine tool.

- Experiment with different strategies and techniques, try out new ideas, and do not be afraid to be creative. Remember businesses are different and campaign goals are also different. Seasons and trends also change.

- Try to be dynamic and original. Create high-quality content that will make your audience feel valued. This will give you more followers and leads for your brand.

Twitter is a goldmine which you can tap to expand your business. Make sure you use the strategies effectively to market your brands on Twitter.

Twitter Marketing Hacks

The main goal of launching Twitter campaigns is to get more audience and to convert the audience into leads. However, achieving this goal may seem like an uphill task if you don't know how to maneuver your ways on Twitter.

You need to grasp the simple hacks that are essential for your Twitter marketing journey.

The Best and Worst Times to Tweet

People access Twitter on computers and mobile devices. This may be in their workplace or at home. The time people spend on this platform also varies between individuals.

So, what is the best time to post your tweets?

Noon to 1.00 p.m. local time. This is the most popular time to post tweets. On average, many people tweet between 11.00 a.m. to 1.00 p.m. with optimum tweets around noon and 1.00 p.m.

Users post fewer tweets between 3.00 and 4.00 a.m. To earn the most clicks, post your tweets around 12 midnight and 3 a.m. Send tweets between 2.00 and 3.00 a.m. for the highest number of clicks.

It is important to note that there are other factors that influence the number of clicks. Posting at 2.00 a.m. may lead to higher clicks once in a while depending on the factors on the number of followers you have, the quality of your content, and day of the week.

Approaches you can use to find the best time to tweet

It is actually possible to determine the exact time

that suits your brand the most. Let us look at four approaches you can use for this purpose:

1. The data-driven approach

This is where you collect data to determine when your audience is most active on Twitter, then post your tweets based on the data collected. Simply post different tweets at different times of the day, then settle on the time that gets you the most engagement.

2. The tools-based approach

You can use tools such as the Tweroid, Follower Wonk, and Audisense to find the best times to tweet.

3. The research-backed approach

You can also base your timing on results from the various research. It is, however, important to note that it is not easy to lock down when the best time to post is, because of the dynamism of Twitter users, trends, and business niches.

4. The "What do the pros do?" approach

Learning from other successful brands is another approach you can use to determine the best time to tweet.

Following successful brands in your industry will give you a clue of how frequently they post and the time of the day that gives them the most engagement.

Grow your Twitter following fast with relevant Twitter followers.

How many Twitter followers do you have? Do you feel there is need to put a little more effort into attracting more followers?

Simple steps you can use to get more twitter followers:

5. Tweet more often when in doubt

Twitter requires an aggressive content strategy to be more effective. Data from CoSchedule affirms that three to seven tweets every day leads to maximum engagement on your account.

Make sure that your content is flexible and tackles various topics such as breaking news, relevant industry articles, and personal updates. This will give your audience a wide variety to read from compared to when you base your content on self-promotion alone.

There is just so much to talk about. So, stop annoying your audience with the same content every time. Posting different content gives the impression that you are active, serious, and you really know what you are doing. This may just earn you more followers and leads for your business.

6. *Time your Tweet to Perfection*

Tweeting when your audience is not active will not gain you any new followers. You need to study your audience to determine when they are most active. This will enable you to tweet at the most appropriate time to allow maximum engagement.

7. Post more visual content

People have a short attention span. Besides, there are many tweets that require their engagement. This is why you should find the most appropriate way to stand out from the crowd and get their attention. The visuals may just be the perfect way of achieving this mission.

Tweets with visual content will give you more likes, shares, and retweets than the tweets without any image. Images are more enticing and trigger the need to have a look at the content.

You can upload images from your computer or use infographic images. Make sure that the image you use is relevant, entertaining, and clear to grab your audience' attention.

8. Master the Arts of Tagging, Retweeting, and Replying

You do not need to spend the whole day on your Twitter account to get more followers. All you need is quality time on the platform.

You can totally schedule your tweets to optimize engagement. However, this will give an impression that your account is run by robots. You need to interact with your followers and other leaders in the industry.

Tags, retweets, likes, and quick response reassures new followers that you are actually human. This will keep them interested in your content. Give detailed and thoughtful feedback. They are more effective than a one or two-word reply.

Tag other brands in the industry to show love. This will grab their attention and make them interested in your content. They may shout you out as well. This is a perfect way to create a business network.

Retweeting your followers gives the potential followers the impression that you are willing to engage with them. This will introduce you to new followers.

9. *Find followers within your network*

Sync your contact list to Twitter to tap into your existing contacts who are most likely to follow you. You should import your email contacts to find new followers on Twitter.

If your contacts have Twitter accounts, the synced account will show up a suggestion under the "who to follow" icon. This is a great strategy to grow your follower list depending on the size of your contact list.

10.   Funnel followers beyond Twitter

You need to promote your account beyond the platform. Link your Twitter account to other related social profiles like Facebook or Instagram to give your followers a wide range of avenues to contact you when the need arises.

You can also include a link to your social encounter on-site next to your opt-in form.

11. Optimize your profile for new followers.

Up to 15% of tweets are bots. You need to do

everything humanly possible to prove to your target audience that you are human.

Below are the approaches you can use to make your content friendlier to the new audience:

- Use a clear profile photo to reassure the audience that you are real. An unobstructed facial photo is preferred.

- Have a complete profile. Describe what you do, your title, your company, and your location.

- Give your followers a taste of your personality.

- Besides the short introductory sentence about your company, you can also promote the specific campaigns you are starting, your top content, or a landing page on the bio. This will enable your audience to make informed decisions.

12. Use hashtags appropriately

A hashtag gives your audience a clue of your content. Tweets with at least one hashtag get 12.6% more engagement than tweets without any hashtag. However, you should not weigh down your post with a lot of unnecessary hashtags.

Use Twitter analytics to determine the top-performing tags for your business niche. You can tack on a number of hashtags to any given tweet to make it easy for new followers to find you.

13. Link out to influencers in your tweet

Naturally, there are people in your industry who have great influence over your target audience. Getting their attention is a great step toward ensuring that you tap the large audience that they control.

You can notify the influencers about the link via Twitter, Google, or email.

14. Use Triberr

Triberr gives your content priority over other content in your followers' feeds. This means that your followers will be able to see your content first before they can see other contents.

15. *Provide value*

This largely depends on your target audience. Provide something that will be beneficial to the followers. This will entice and encourage them to be part of your promotion.

16. *Provide contests*

People like free stuff. A contest is a great way to capitalize on this habit. You have to put in more effort if your goal extends beyond getting more followers.

More attention should be given to:

- Simplicity- Make the process of participating in the contest simple to encourage more people to participate. Give clear instructions on the requirements and the procedure your audience should use to join the contest.

- Integrate user content generation- Encourage the audience to submit user-generated content in the contest to make it more interesting.

- Choose an appropriate price- Avoid giving products from other companies as prizes. This is to ensure that you close all loopholes of losing your clients to such companies in the future.

- Avoid the annoying spammy promotions- Keep it simple and clear. If you must go overboard, minimize the promotional Tweets. You should focus more on value rather than increasing followers. Your followers will feel that you have their best interest in mind.

Growing real Twitter followers takes time and effort. Any shortcut may lead to your account being closed by the Twitter support team. Use the simple tips we have discussed to grow your Twitter followers.

Get more engagement with your Tweets

Getting enough deal on Twitter is the real deal. There are simple techniques that you can use to get more engagements.

They include:

1. *Keep your tweets below 110 characters*

People have a short attention span. Limit your posts to under 110 characters to encourage your followers to read your content. Shorter tweets also leave room for your followers to retweet your tweet.

2. *Tweet during the day*

Research shows that most Twitter audience is active during the day. Tweet between 8 am and 7 pm to get a higher engagement.

3. *Share images*

Tweets with images are more appealing and leave memorable impacts than ordinary tweets. Add relevant images to your tweet to grab the attention of your followers and keep them hooked by your content.

4. Include links

Clicking on links contributes to 92% of all Twitter engagement. Provide links to make it easy for your followers to interact with you.

5. Keep off lifestyle tweets

Use Twitter as a professional marketing platform. Avoid tweeting about personal-life journal because you are a brand, not a celebrity.

6. Use strong calls to action

Make your call to action strong, precise, and valuable to grab more attention. Your call to action should focus on the value the readers will get.

7. Send up to 4 tweets a day

As a brand, you need to be careful about coming too strong with your marketing. Limit your tweeting and instead concentrate more on engaging with your followers through replies, retweets, and likes.

8. Use hashtags

Use hashtags to create more visibility for your brand on Twitter.

9. Ask for retweets

Don't shy away from asking your followers to retweet your tweet. Make sure that you spell out the word retweet in its entirety.

Drive More Traffic to your Website

Unknown to many people, Twitter is a great source of traffic for websites. You need to build your Twitter presence and connect with your audience effectively. This will help to evangelize your brand to your prospects and potential clients.

Below are tips for captivating a Twitter presence for your brand:

1. Use hashtags

Hashtags give you more engagement which leads to more followers on your Twitter account.

2. Avatar, Background, and Bio

Tell people who you are and what your business is about to help them have a clue of what they are following.

You need to design the background of your Twitter profile to reflect your ideas. Use a facial photo of yourself or the logo of your company.

3. Don't set your tweets to private

Shielding your Twitter account from the general public will only get you a few followers. Make your account public so that a large audience from different sources can access it.

4. Tweet at the right time

Tweet your best content during peak times to get more retweets and engagement from your followers.

5. Track your results

Keep records of your new followers to help you engage with them effectively.

6. Links to your Twitter page

Provide links to your website and other social profiles like Facebook to give your followers more avenue to find you and communicate with you.

Twitter provides a great opportunity to build a strong online presence. Give your audience valuable content to trigger their desire to find your website and participate in your online marketing campaign.

Effectively Use Hashtags on Twitter

A hashtag is a combination of a pound sign (#) in front of the keywords without any space, for example, #MotivateMonday. Hashtags are clickable making it possible for users to be directed to all other content related to the hashtag.

Hashtags are powerful tools for Twitter marketing as they make it possible to have quick engagements with your followers.

6 ways you can use hashtags on Twitter for maximum traffic creation:

1. *Check the Trends*

Find the keywords or phrases that are currently trending. Search for the keyword in the search.Twitter.com. This will show you the number of times the keyword has been used.

If it has only been used for a few engagements, then it is worth trying it out as the competition is still low.

2. *Use Branded Keywords*

Hashtags with branded keywords will make your tweets stand out from the crowd. When your follower links on the branded keyword, he will know all the conversations that are tweeted using that particular hashtag.

Branded keywords will result in more activities on your Twitter page leading to more traffic and leads for the brand.

3. *Relevancy*

Providing relevant content is one of the best ways to command many followers on Twitter. Hashtags are not exempted when it comes to relevancy.

You need to ensure that the keywords you use in the hashtag are relevant and provide value to your audience. Relevance will help you to attract many followers who will gladly click, retweet, or like your content.

4. *Avoid using too many hashtags*

You don't need to flood your tweets with unnecessary hashtags. Two or three hashtags should be enough to achieve the desired effect. Do not forget that the characters you should use are limited.

Too many hashtags will make your post appear as

spammy and may give the impression that you do not know what you are doing. Just keep it simple and sweet for maximum engagement with your followers.

You can use the hashtags in the beginning, in between your posts, or at the end of the post depending on your content. Avoid lengthy hashtags as this may be difficult to read that confuse your followers. A hashtag with one or two words is more effective.

5. *Don't use hashtags to promote your own brand*

Self-promotion will give the impression that you are trying so hard to create awareness about your products. Other marketers will also accuse you of starting an artificial grassroots movement.

6. *Set focused goals and monitor your performance*

It is important to have a clear goal in mind before launching the Twitter campaign. This will enable you to create hashtags that are geared towards achieving the goals.

There is no one fit-all hashtag for all Twitter campaigns. Test the various hashtags to determine which hashtag layout gives you the maximum engagement with your followers.

Hashtags are powerful tools in Twitter marketing. Hashtags make it possible to have quick engagements with your followers, they provide instant traffic as well as opening doors for many people to find and connect with your brand.

You can use tools such as Twitter search, Hashtagify, Trends Map, and Keyhole to find and utilize popular hashtags.

Use Twitter Lists the Right Way

Twitter lists allow you to effectively interact with the different audience segment. They help brands to save a lot of time to sift through feeds and search for new users.

You can use the list to increase engagement with your clients, other influencers, and partners without having to send them tweets or messages.

Below are 6 ways you can use the Twitter list to grow your brand:

- ***Monitor competitors***

Keeping a record of your competitors' accounts makes it easy to monitor their tweets and activities. You can also monitor their updates and offers so that you find better ways to stay ahead of them always.

It is possible to privatize your Twitter list so that your competitors will not realize that you are monitoring them.

- ***Connect with industry leaders***

Have one powerful list to record industry leaders. You can manage and improve your relationship with the industry leader using the list.

Follow their tweets to know what they are up to.

This will enable you to engage with them more confidently in a consistent manner. You can share the list with your followers and encourage them to subscribe.

This will make your account a valuable resource which followers look up to for useful information.

- ***Stay on Top of Trends***

Create a list to keep up with the latest trends and news on Twitter without getting distracted. Have a list of websites and users who constantly share the latest trends and news.

You also need to find out-of-the-box sources and upcoming news sites for a unique and fresh list.

- ***Engage with employees***

An employee list will encourage your employees to know and understand each other better. You can easily integrate new employees into an existing team for better performance.

Include the list link in your Twitter bio to

encourage your followers to interact with your employees as well.

- ***Reward your biggest fans***

Create a list of your most active followers. Engage with these followers regularly by showing them love, sharing their tweets, mentioning them and thanking them often.

This is a positive reinforcement that increases the chances of them continuing to share your content and act as your loyal customers.

You can also use this list to find out the sources of your most active users. This will enable you to have a great plan to tap other potential followers for the growth of your business.

- ***Maintain customer relationships***

The way you handle your customers can either break you or grow your brand. Many people who cannot access your business physically may resort to reaching you via your Twitter page.

You need to have an effective social media management team who will provide relevant and engaging responses to the users' inquiries.

When other users mention or tag you, add them to your Twitter list and start engaging with them as soon as possible.

Creating a list will improve your Twitter experience. It is however not an overnight activity. Develop the list, nurture it, and give it time to grow and bring more success to your business.

Using Twitter Polls for Marketing

Twitter polls are native polls used for collecting feedback and giving people the opportunity to weigh in on questions.

Below are ways you can use Twitter polls as your marketing strategy:

1. *Guide your content decisions*

Use feedback from your followers to help you to

create great and valuable content for the followers.

2. Establish thought leadership

Create a poll about leading topics in your industry to establish your brand as a thought leader.

3. Involve your followers in brand decisions

Listen to the opinions and contributions of your followers regarding your brand to build loyalty and trust. Your followers will feel strongly connected with your brand when you show them that you care about them and their opinions.

4. Add hashtags

Include branded or trending hashtags to increase your visibility on Twitter.

5. Repurpose content type

Create Twitter polls around lengthy and useful content to drive continued awareness about the topic.

6. *Make it simple*

Make your Twitter polls simple so that people can easily engage with you directly. Less complicated polls will give you the desired feedback about your products as it will encourage your followers to air out their opinions.

7. *Promote your products and services*

Twitter poll makes it easy to promote your products and services as it makes the promotion appear like entertainment rather than the spammy advertisements.

8. *Set the appropriate end date*

Set your Twitter polls to end when the topic is still relevant and useful to your followers. The end date can be between 5 minutes and 7 days depending on the length and value of your content.

Learn to listen to the opinions of your consumers

as this will present you with new and better ways to engage with your current and potential customers. These hacks should help guide you through the Twitter marketing campaign for the most optimal performance and results.

Chapter 4 : Pinterest Marketing

You must have had a pin board when you were younger, maybe even still do. And you put photos there, of memories you have made, things you would like to see more often and such things. Some tend to have the door of their fridge as such a makeshift pin board and they stick photos and images on it.

Pinterest is quite similar to this. It is a sort of virtual pin board where you can put images on. It is made even better because, unlike a physical pin board, you can group your images into different categories, and add as many images as you like. It is completely visual which means you can't post content unless there's an image in the content.

You basically find the image and video content that you like on the internet and you can curate it. This differs from other social media where you keep your own images since it emphasizes on discovering images other than your own to pin to your boards.

Other than that, you can also connect with friends and family or just other Pinterest users through the site by liking and commenting on their images, or re-pinning those they have pinned. It is a free social media site, so you get to open your account at no extra cost.

Pinterest Background

Pinterest has been gaining traction ever since its inception in 2010. It currently has over 150 million active users despite being fairly new which makes it a fast-growing social network. It has become a major medium for sharing visual content, competing with other social media giants like Instagram.

Studies have shown that it is more popular amongst women, with about 60% of Pinterest users being female. This may be attributed to the fact that when it first started, Pinterest was used mainly to share content on themes that are more popular with ladies like fashion, cooking, and gardening.

Over the years it has, however, spread its wings to other interests that are bound to have more men joining.

Today there are very diverse interests being shown on the platform, including more of those considered more attractive to part of the male population like archery and hunting. This should see an increase in the number of men using the site.

Common terms around Pinterest

- Pinning: This refers to sharing or posting content on the platform.

- Board: The board is like the physical board that you can pin things on. It is where you pin your virtual images. You can have several of them and group them according to different themes.

- Re-pin: This is when a user shares an image

you have pinned on their board. It is the equivalent of re-tweeting on Twitter.

You can find images to pin within the site from other people's boards. Alternatively, you can share images that you find on your browser through Pinterest, or manually upload images to Pinterest using the icon as well. Pinterest also allows you to share pins on other social networks like Facebook and Twitter.

You can use the site to showcase your products in a creative and appealing manner. A quick browse through the site will have you notice the use of color and good quality images to appeal to the audience. The more attractive your images are, the more likely you are to have more people noticing your account.

Pinterest is used by many different professionals such as photographers and retailers who showcase different images meant to promote their work. It can be used as a portfolio for the photographer or product catalog for the retailer.

Have your products shown in an appealing manner to get the attention of the audiences.

If you have a vast array of products, the boards come in handy to divide the items into different categories. Have different boards for items in the different groups and give them topics that are searchable so people can find them easily.

If you have several interests, like a retail shop and photography, dividing the content into different boards may also work for you.

The re-pinning feature is also quite helpful to marketers as it allows users to share content they love from your account with friends and this further promotes your brand. The users can also comment on items they love.

Other features that may come in handy for you include the community sharing features. Here, you have the ability to choose who can pin content on your board. This may be great to connect with potential clients as they can share pins on your boards. You can choose admins to pin content to certain boards and have community boards to encourage user engagement.

Get inspired

The large reservoir of image and video content available on the site is also great for you. It may act as the inspiration you need, giving you ideas on how to present your brand.

You may get new ways of promoting your products as well as other content that you can share on your boards. Just browse through different collections within and outside of your niche and get inspired.

Seeing as it is a fairly easy site to use and with a lot of potential for businesses, it might be time to go beyond the common social media sites and try Pinterest out to increase your social media outreach.

How Pinterest Works: The different functionalities

Pinterest is used as a medium for discovering and exchanging different ideas. There is a range of themes for the different ideas, and you can find almost anything you are looking for from animal images to recipes that you can try out, different electronic devices and their usage, or even clothing items.

It is quite easy to use and understand Pinterest. You already have a general idea of what it is from Chapter 1 of this book; a large pin board that you can use to pin your ideas on. And these ideas can be seen by other people as well as get comments from them.

Is Pinterest a Social Media Network?

Although it is more of a search engine for visual content, we can say that it is a social media channel because of its social aspects. Unlike other search engines, Pinterest doesn't only allow searches for different items. It also includes engagement between users by liking and commenting on other people's content as well as following certain users and even sharing content from other users.

So, How Does It Work?

To fully know how exactly Pinterest works, and take full advantage of what it has to offer, you will first need to create an account. This allows you to get access to all features including the social side of the app.

To start on the site, you will need to either search for it and use the web version of it or download the app on your mobile device, whether Android or iOS.

Getting Started

Once you have access to Pinterest, you can start the signing up process. It is completely free and only uses up a few minutes of your time before you are good to go.

To sign up, choose your preferred option,

whether you want to sign up with your email address or Facebook or Twitter account. Signing up for Facebook or Twitter lets you connect your Pinterest account to the other accounts. This makes it easier to connect with friends and family, as well as other users that may be of interest to you based on who you follow or are friends with on the other sites.

In case you do not sign up using Facebook or Twitter, do not worry. You can always link the accounts up later. You will need to continue with the sign-up process by keying in your personal information including your name, email address, and gender.

For one who has chosen to sign up using Facebook or Twitter, you will enter your login credentials and then the site will access account information needed for your sign up. This includes email address, friends list, and any other information that is basic and easily available.

Generate a strong password for your account.

Once you have done all this, the next step will be verification. Here, you will receive an email in the account you registered with. Open this email to click on the confirmation prompt to verify your account.

Setting up your Profile

Finish setting up your account by heading to settings. To find the settings icon, navigate to the profile icon at the top right corner of the taskbar for one using the desktop site. On the app, the profile icon is found in the bottom left corner of the screen.

Once there, click on the 'bolt' icon where you will find the settings. Edit your profile at will. You may, for instance, include a bio, a profile photo, as well as location to further improve your account's look. This is also the place to change your privacy settings and notifications settings. You can also link your profile to other sites like Facebook and Google+ here.

For notifications, you can keep email

notifications on, to begin with. This allows you to see the kind of interaction your pins are getting and know who likes your content. You can follow some of these people and find more targeted content for them. Later on, when the notifications increase and become too much, you can turn off email notifications.

While setting up your profile, consider other social media sites that you are already in. The username should be similar across all your social media accounts to make it easier for people to find you. Also, stick to a theme on all social media sites, to enable easier recognition by your followers, and ease in finding you when they conduct a search on Pinterest.

You may have the same profile photo to avoid confusion as well. The aim is to get people knowing who you are at first glance, especially if they have seen your brand on another social network.

Posting Content from the Web

The next thing you need to know is how to post content on Pinterest. Posting image or video content is known as pinning. You pin the content on a board from various sources. You can add content from your device or from the web.

To add content from different sites you visit, you can use different ways depending on the site visited. Some websites usually have the option of sharing on Pinterest. Look out for the Pin It button on the sites, usually next to share buttons for other sites like Facebook and Twitter.

If that option isn't there, you can try going to the three dots on your browser, and clicking on the share button, then 'Pin It' button. You may need to install this 'Pin It' button to your web browser. Head on to the 'Goodies' page on Pinterest to get instructions on how to install the 'Pin It' button.

Pinning Content

So how do you pin the content to your boards? While on a website you are visiting, click on the

'Pin It' button. If there are several images or videos, then there should be a pop-up that comes up where you can select the image you would like to share. Select the image you are interested in then create the pin as prompted.

At this stage, you can choose a board to pin the image on and also add descriptions to the pin. Descriptions should be aimed at explaining the image and its context so that you can remember why you pinned the image, and your viewers will also have some background information on it. Choose the board that has similar images or create a new one for that particular image.

Creating a new Board

Pinterest allows you to have several different boards to pin on. You can categorize the boards into different themes or products. To create a new board, find the 'Add+' icon which is usually found at the top right corner of your Pinterest page.

You can then add a board and have a name that

describes what you will pin there. While coming up with a descriptive title for your board, find one that will easily inform any visitors what to expect from that board in particular.

Once you have created your board, you will be given the option to add another pinner to it. This refers to another user who can pin items on the board together with you. The board will, therefore, be shared. Add other pinners to your board to make it easier to share diverse content, but ensure it is within the category the board is under.

Re-pinning Content

It is also possible to re-pin content that has been pinned by other users. If you like a certain user's pin, for instance, hover over the specific image and look out for the three buttons. You will see a re-pin button amongst these and you can click on it and then choose amongst your boards for the one to pin the image on.

You can encourage users to re-pin your content

as a way of promoting your brand and products. Re-pinning other users' images also creates a good rapport with the audience.

User Engagement

You can engage with other users on Pinterest by using the liking and commenting feature. There is a like button that lets one like images they find interesting on Pinterest. The owner of the pin will see this step.

Users also have the ability to comment on your pins. There is a comment button that allows one to take this step. Look out for pins that other users have liked and commented on your boards to know which create most user engagement.

Pinterest Following

You may be curious as to how people following you on Pinterest will affect your marketing. Should you focus on getting as many people as you can to follow you like on other social media channels?

A good following is great for any social media site for the fact that it gives you an audience for any content shared. It also provides a substantial social proof. However, it would be good to note that people who follow you won't always see everything you pin on your boards in their newsfeeds.

For this reason, followers may not be the most important aspect of Pinterest. Instead, try to make it Search Engine Optimized instead. It should be easy to search for and find your pins. Focus on getting as much traffic as you can from Pinterest.

Pinterest Business Account

Since your main aim is to use Pinterest for marketing, consider opening a business account. The account provides you with detailed analytics on how your account is performing. This enables you to plan out your campaigns accordingly for maximum impact. You are also able to advertise more easily with a business account while getting all the services of a personal account.

Other Features

There are several other features that you may not know of and which could be of great help to your marketing endeavors.

Board Widgets

Did you know you could include widgets for specific boards on your website or blogs? On your website, you may have content on different products or services that you offer. You can have a widget that represents a specific board along with the other share buttons on your website.

When having this widget, choose a board that is most relevant to the topic on that particular web page. This allows site visitors to be directed straight to the most relevant board on your account and may increase your followers.

Page Widgets

You have seen them on other websites, those small widgets that show the website's owner is on Pinterest. This would be a great addition to your site so that visitors can follow you on Pinterest as well or visit your profile using this widget. To add a page widget, go to your 'About' section and get clear instructions on how to go about it.

Group Boards

This feature allows more than one pinner to pin items on a board, unlike the other boards where only the account owner can pin content. If you opt for this sort of board, you will need to keep tabs on the activity on it. There might be irrelevant content on there that would show a negative outlook, and you may lose followers over this.

You can get to group board settings and turn on email notifications for select groups that may have irrelevant content. This should help you keep a handle on the shared content.

Pinterest Sharing Feature

Pinterest has the option of sending pins to email contacts and your friends on Facebook, amongst others. You can even go a step further and add a personalized message to the pin before sharing it.

This creates many possibilities for you, as you can send pins to potential clients. Have pins that are informative or helpful in a way to the life of an individual to share with them. It should benefit them in one way or the other to ensure you capture their attention.

Pinterest serves several functions as seen from this chapter. Its features all serve different purposes for the site. We have seen some of the features that are especially good for businesses and marketers like the page and board widgets as well as Pinterest analytics feature.

Use this knowledge on Pinterest to further your marketing campaigns on the site. Also, be on the lookout for any upgrades and inclusion of more features that could aid your marketing strategies and take full advantage of what it has to offer.

How to Use Pinterest for Marketing and to Earn Money

Social media sites have become a hot hub for marketing as well as earning money. Businesses and marketers are streaming into these platforms to take advantage of the opportunities presented by social media.

Each site, from Facebook to Instagram, Snapchat and Pinterest, amongst others, provides unique benefits and platforms that you can use for your marketing purposes. Since they all have different potentials, you will need to be well-versed in each of them and which ways to gain the most from them.

Pinterest is one of the platforms that is still not yet fully understood by many in terms of its marketing potential. Many assume that it is used just to have people look at exotic destinations they would like to visit; DIY crafts they can try out and feed their obsessions of flowers or pet photos. But that is not all as we will find out.

Strategies and Tips for Pinterest Marketing

Let us look at the possibilities of marketing on Pinterest and find out strategies and tips we can use to market on the platform or earn money from it.

1. Open a Pinterest Business Account

The very first step to marketing is getting a business account. It is different from the personal account in that it has more features that are optimized for businesses. Once you get your Pinterest business account, do take note of the different terms of service that come with the account.

Do not rush into using promotion techniques you use on other social media sites like:

- Promoting spam. You need to stay away from asking other users to comment every other time.

- Having frequent contests. You might be

tempted to have contests where people have to re-pin a specific pin to enter the contests, and the one with the highest number of likes wins. While a similar contest is okay on sites like Facebook and Twitter, Pinterest discourages its users from such.

- Expecting Pinterest to Sponsor or endorse your business in any way.

There are more of these and you can access them on the Pinterest terms of service once you create a business account. Try to stick to these guidelines for the best experience. And not to worry, just because you can't use the same techniques that worked with other social media sites doesn't mean Pinterest will not work for you.

There are several features that are exclusive to a Pinterest business account. These include:

a) Pinterest Analytics

With a business account, you get access to

Pinterest analytics. Pinterest provides you with insights on how your pins are performing. This feature is quite amazing as it gives you a way to track your pins.

Use this feature to see which sort of content and strategies are working as well as which are not. You can use the information you get from Pinterest analytics to plan out different marketing strategies and find ways that work for you.

b) Business Name

With a personal account, you are restricted to having a First Name-Last Name combination as your user name. A business account however lets you use the name of your business, and you can have a same business name across all social media sites including Pinterest.

c) Rich pins

Normal pins usually have very little information. You can however use this feature to add more information to your pins including prices if the pins are of products, links, and such other valuable information. This allows for an increase in sales ability and makes your pins more visible and able to generate traffic.

There are several strategies you can put in place to have more successful Pinterest campaigns. The aim is to create engagement with your pins and have more people seeing them. So how can you achieve this?

1. *Link all your Social Media platforms*

When you start out on Pinterest, there is no need to start gaining followers from scratch. Simply connect your other social media accounts to Pinterest. This gives you access to your followers on other sites who are also on Pinterest. It lets even more people see your content as they will see the content on whichever site they are on.

Linking up your social media accounts also adds the different buttons like Facebook and Twitter to your Pinterest. You will need to have a personal Facebook account to link up as pages cannot be linked to Pinterest.

2. Create Searchable Pins

Pinterest is a sort of visual search engine. It is like a Google for Images, as you can literally search for images or videos on anything on the site. Most people tend to do just that; search for images of modern kitchens for instance and get a whole list of images under this search term.

Like written content where you use every way to ensure your content is searchable, the pins you put on the site also need to be searchable. You should be working towards having people land on your profile when they search for anything similar to what you offer. Make your content searchable by:

3. Use Popular Pinterest Categories

You can tell which categories are most popular by doing a simple search. Some of the most popular categories include DIY pins. Your work is to have boards meant for pins that fall under the most popular categories.

However, do not just pick any category because of its popularity amongst users. Ensure it is in line with your industry and that it can work for you. Depending on the relevance to your business and what you offer, you can pick which categories to place your boards under. Accordingly, popular categories should guide you in creating your boards.

4. Have Quality Pins

Pinterest is a very visual site as you must have seen while going over it. The sort of content you place there is therefore crucial to your whole marketing campaign. The images you pin on your boards form the backbone of your account.

While coming up with content to share on this platform, aim for images that will have an impact on the users of Pinterest. Use images to sell your brand to the audience and make them appealing. Consider the size and quality of an image before sharing it.

5. *Have a Perfect Image Size*

The size of the image can vary depending on the image or your preference. Generally, the width is usually constant for all pins. The difference comes in the length. You can have an extra-long image or a shorter one. Aim for a medium sized image. You can use different templates to make the work of getting your images to a perfect size easier.

Instructographics

The name comes from the nature of such images which are used mostly to show step by step instructions of doing or creating something. They are images that are longer in size and are especially popular with DIY pins. If a particular pin is not a how-to guide, do avoid these longer images.

6. *Timely Posting of Pins*

Once you have created great content to pin, you

will then need to have as many people seeing the pin as possible. Try not to pin at any random time; instead, choose the time wisely by going for a time when you are most likely to reach a lot of people.

This time is referred to as an optimal posting time. It is convenient because at that time there are most likely more people on the site compared to the rest of the day. To find the optimal posting time, you will need to understand your audience.

You can try out different times that you think are the best and then find out which brings the most engagement. You will need to understand your audience to get the best time. To begin with you can try afternoon hours or mid-morning hours. Avoid late night and very early morning posting as very few people are awake at that time or online anyway.

7. Frequent Pinning

How often should one share pins on Pinterest, every other week? Should you post just one every other day or go all out and post several of them a day?

Frequency of posting tends to play a role in gaining more followers for your account. Post at least five pins every other day to remain relevant. If you can post 20 plus pins, then do so. When posting pins, you can re-pin content pinned by others, but also ensure that most of the content is your own unique content.

Do not post all of them at the same time, as this makes the whole reason behind frequent pins useless. Space your posts such that you are posting them at different times of the day; this helps you reach more people as they are more likely to see at least one of your posts.

8. Search Engine Optimization

Optimizing your pins for search engines is another strategy you need to put in place to further marketing using the site. This makes it easier to search, and you will be more accessible to people. You can do this by using Keywords.

There are tools to help you get great keyword combinations that you can use together with your pins. Use tools like Google AdWords to search for keywords relevant to your industry. Once you find keywords you can use, add them to the pins, and you can add them in different places for instance:

- Pin titles. The keywords will appear on the titles of the pins.

- File names. Add these keywords to the names of the image or video files.

- Pin Descriptions. Where you put in the descriptions of the pins, add the keywords there as well.

While employing the use of keywords, take care not to go overboard with them. Use them in as natural a way as possible. For instance, in a description, instead of just using the keywords, have a contextually relevant description of the image with the keywords added such that it fits seamlessly and sounds less like the work of a robot.

Using the right keywords will lead people to your pins more easily as long as they search for content using your keywords. Optimizing your Pinterest for search is quite easy.

9. *Engage with other Users*

Engaging with other Pinterest users is important to grow on the platform. You will need to build a relationship with other people that might be potential clients or partners in future. You can take part in different forms of user engagement.

a. Reply to Comments

This should be the most obvious step. When a user comments on your pin, they show interest in what you have to offer.

The worst thing you could do is not respond to the comments, as it will look like bad customer service. You want to show them you care and that you are willing to help, so make sure you answer any questions asked.

An added advantage would be to personalize your responses and use their names while addressing them.

b. Show some Love on their pins

Another avenue that you can engage with Pinterest users on is by commenting on and liking their posts.

Look out for your followers' posts and leave comments on them as well. One or two comments on your followers' pins will leave them feeling more connected to you.

Commenting on followers' boards also puts you out there for their followers to see. You get easy marketing of your brand with this step while creating good relations with your followers.

c. Follow Popular Boards

Are there popular boards within your industry or something close? You can gain a lot by following them and engaging with them as well.

By following them, you get to see what they pin, their frequency of sharing pins, engagement levels, and other techniques they use. You can borrow ideas from such to adopt in your own marketing strategies.

Commenting on some of their pins every once in a while, also serve to promote your brand. Remember they have a huge following, and many people will see your comments and possibly go ahead to visit your profile.

Follow boards that are relevant in your industry. This way you will attract more targeted traffic to your profile and the strategies used to showcase the boards will be even more useful to you.

10. Use the Open Board

Have a board where you allow multiple Pinterest users to post their own pins. This creates a sort of community by allowing other users to contribute to your Pinterest account. The other users cannot change the name or description of the board but can pin content on it.

Work at getting influencers or leaders to pin content on your board. This makes for great brand promotion. Use the open board to increase interaction between users and your brand.

11. Use Rich Pins

You can use rich pins to add more information to your pins. Rich pins increase the probability of people visiting your site. Some of the available rich pins that can be beneficial to your business account include:

Product Pins – you can add the product price, the location of a store, as well as stock availability.

Article Pins – Add a headline, author's name, and description of an article related to the pin.

Place Pins – These allow one to add location on maps, addresses, and other contact information.

App Pins – These are new and only available for IOS. They enable users to install an app on the Pinterest site without leaving it.

12. Add Links to your Website or Blog

To bring traffic to your website from Pinterest, you will need to add a link in the description. You can add a link to pins that do not need other information like addresses or product pins.

13. Post Diverse content

Do not use Pinterest solely as a catalog to show your products on. Have different content other than product images. You can have relevant quotes or show products in their contexts. This makes your account more interesting to viewers.

14. Add Pin It Buttons on your Sites

If someone is on your site, it should be easy for them to further interact with you on Pinterest. To enable this, you can add a 'Pin It button' to images present on your website or blog.

Visitors can pin your images on their boards or visit your account for more. They encourage even more interaction on your Pinterest account.

Making Money from Pinterest

You can make money on Pinterest by using the strategies for marketing to market a product or service that you offer. Following these strategies will lead to an increase in sales.

Affiliate Marketing – Partner with a company to promote their product and sell it for a part of the profit the product will garner. Ensure what you market is in tandem with your other content to maintain relevance.

Finally, Pinterest has many benefits and using the mentioned strategies will ensure that you gain from it.

Chapter 5 : YouTube SEO Best Practices

Online marketing has changed the face of marketing. It has been used time and again by advertisers to reach the large number of internet users that are on the internet surfing every other day. The content by marketers has been optimized in different ways in a bid to set themselves apart from competing companies.

The content of the advertisements was earlier only in written form, like blog posts and eBooks, amongst others. However, it was later discovered that video content is the most popular amongst internet users. This presented an opportunity for advertisers to tap into the world of marketing by sound and video such as through podcasts, GIFs, and videos.

With the large number of people consuming video content such as on YouTube, there has been a need to get it right. This brings us to the

YouTube SEO best practices to ensure that advertisements placed on YouTube are actually successful.

The best thing about video content is that it is easy for the internet user to see. It does not take much time or effort like written content. Most people would prefer to watch a video over reading, and it sticks in one's mind. This makes it a must have for the online marketer. So how do you optimize your videos for search?

Tips for YouTube search Optimization

There are different ways in which you can improve your video campaign on YouTube to be more easily visible and have more people landing on your advert in the search results page. All things play a part in reaching out to viewers to compel them to watch your video, from the very first time they get to the search page, working together to have one watch the video, take an interest in the product being promoted, and take the next step where they become a client for your business.

1. Relevant Title

The title is one of the most important things for a good YouTube video campaign. Just look at it in a practical manner; when you search for a video, the title is what you see first. It is also the point at which you decide whether you will click on that video or not. The title draws you in or has you looking elsewhere.

As the first point of appeal for the searcher, your title needs to be the kind that will have people clicking through. This calls for creativity and specificity. Have a title that not only draws the target audience in, but is also clear and straight to the point.

The title should also be similar to the viewer's search objectives. This means the keywords should match with the title, so that the viewer gets exactly what they searched for in the title alone.

You may get carried away in formulating the title, and have a long one so as to incorporate every bit of information you deem necessary within it. The problem with this is that your title is at jeopardy of being cut short when it appears in the search results page. You do not want this so keep your title short and concise.

2. Written Description

YouTube videos provide for a brief description of your video in written form. The key word here should be 'brief.' Ensure that your description is brief and that it does not resemble a short story or blog. The people you are targeting are there for the video, not a whole lot of words.

YouTube usually allows 1000 characters, but you do not need all these. Have a short, simple description. While writing the description, ensure you put the most important or relevant information first.

Remember YouTube will only show the first few lines on the search results page, and one has to click on the button that indicates 'Show more' to read the rest of the content. This is for if you write a long description. If possible however, have content that will all be displayed on the search results page without further action by the viewer.

3. Video Thumbnail

This refers to the image that appears for the viewers once they land on the search results page. Together with the title and the description, the image is another important aspect for YouTube video marketing.

The thumbnail informs the viewer of what to expect. It is like a snippet of the video content. YouTube does offer images that are auto-generated. You can choose this option and simply pick one. However, having a custom image may be a better option.

Have a good quality image but ensure that it is small enough for easy download. You can use .jpg, .bmp or any other format that allows small size images. Custom thumbnails make your ad more unique and you can choose an image that better represents your company.

It may be good to note that the thumbnail may actually increase the number of clicks on your link by the viewers who land on your advert on the search results page.

4. Use of Tags

Tags act as a way of letting viewers know what the video is about. Apart from informing the viewers, however, tags also play a huge role for YouTube. It uses them to get to know what the content of your video is about and then associate it with similar videos.

Associating your video with similar videos would allow you to have a wider reach as well as get a more targeted audience for your content that is most likely to turn into higher conversions.

While choosing your tags, you need to pay close attention to the specific tags so that you get it right. Start with the most important words and ensure that the tags are relevant to your content. Find words that are commonly used and have them as your tags, ensuring their relevance to your industry and video.

5. Category

You will want your video to appear under a category that has videos with content similar to yours. Categorizing is a way to bring more traffic to your video. To do this, head to the advanced settings option on YouTube and add a category to your uploaded video.

Finding the category for a video might be complicated, especially in getting it right so that it works to your benefit. You can look at the available categories that describe your video and find amongst them one that has an audience that you mean to target, videos with the same quality, length, and value as your own and with creators that are known for something close to yours. With this, you can get the category that will work well for you.

Once you have achieved all this, your video should be able to sell itself such that the traffic that views your advert actually translates to more business for your company. Consider professional input when it comes to the video so that you have good quality content.

YouTube SEO best practices might be the break your company has been waiting for. If you have been stagnant in video marketing, try these tips to improve traffic for your advert and have a higher rate of success.

Chapter 6 : Snapchat Marketing

Snapchat must be a very confusing phenomenon for most, with people wondering what use it is.

Why would you want to post a video or image on a platform only to have it disappear after a while? What is the use of that? Is that all there is to it? Posting disappearing photos?

Yet, with the number of people using it, there must be something more that it offers users. Well, let us look at it, what it is, and how it is used.

If you have never known how to use it and would like to try, stick with us and get to discover how you can do just that.

What is Snapchat?

Snapchat is an app for Android and iOS. As the name suggests, it is an app that allows people to communicate by sharing photos they snap throughout their day.

What sets it apart from other social media sites is that the photos or videos sent to the app are usually available for a while, after which they disappear.

This temporary state of content is what draws people in and calls for a more natural flow of interaction. Mostly, the content is there for 24 hours.

There is a lot you can do with Snapchat, from sharing photos with your followers in what is known as 'stories,' share the photos and videos privately with particular friends, having live video chats, and creating Bitmoji avatars, amongst other things.

Snapchat has changed the face of social media, making it all about instant communication. You send and receive photos and videos on your phone. You do not, however, keep the posts you or your followers share, accumulating them over a while like on other sites.

It boasts over 200 million users, with about half of those being daily active users. The rate of photo sharing is extremely high with about 700 million images shared every other day. This provides quite the audience for your business. It is, therefore, a great tool to add to your marketing strategies.

Snapchat Features

There are several features that make Snapchat what it is. The developers keep upgrading the app every short while, changing things up for it. This makes it hard to have a manual on how to use it as there may be changes made to it, making it work differently.

However, we can look at the features and what each generally does.

1. The Camera

Once you open the Snapchat app, you are taken to the camera screen. This is where you can take a snap or a video to share with your preferred audience.

To take a snap, just tap on the capture button, and if you would like to take a video, press and hold on the same capture button. You can take a video of a maximum of 10 seconds; any longer than that will have your post divided into several snaps.

When you take the snap, you can use the tools that the app avails to you to customize the photo. For instance, you can add a caption to it by tapping on the text tool or tap the pencil icon to draw on the photo as you please. You can save the photo to your memories, send to a friend, or share to the public.

1. Memories

This allows you to view previously saved snaps which you can then edit and share. To open it, just swipe up, or go to the icon below the capture button.

The memories feature lets you access images

saved on Snapchat and also those that were stored locally on your device. Browse through your saved memories through this feature.

2. Stories

This is a critical feature for promotion and marketing strategies as you want to share your content with as many people as possible. It is the feature that lets you share your snaps with your followers.

Once you take a snap, you can tap on the arrow button at the lower left corner of the screen and add it to your story. You can have as many images as you would like and add them all to your story. They will appear in a chronological order for those who see them. They will then disappear after 24 hours.

On the stories screen, you can tap 'My Story' icon and post your story there. To view other people's stories for the purpose of increasing interaction or any other reason, swipe to the left to access the stories screen.

3. Chats

You can chat with people within the app privately or in a group; simply swipe to the right to access the chat screen. If the other party is also present, then you will see a blue dot appearing at the bottom of your screen.

Once every participant leaves a chat, the chat is deleted immediately.

4. Search

This feature is quite important for marketing. You can use it to find topics related to your industry and get to see trends that you can use while getting content to share on Snapchat as well as what your competitors are up to.

To access it, tap on the search icon that usually appears at the top of the camera screen.

5. Editing Tools

The editing tools available on the app give you a chance to customize your photos and videos before sharing them. You can make them stand out by adding emoji, stickers, captions, and even filters to them. Give your audience appealing images and videos to view using this feature.

There are other features like:

- A map that allows you to share your location with your followers. This may be a great feature to use to inform your potential clients where you are based if you have a physical address.

- Settings feature: You can customize the settings as you wish and set up a Snap Code to make it easier for users to follow you.

Snapchat is especially helpful if your target market is a younger generation, the 'millennials,' and even more so if they are female.

How Snapchat Works: The different functionalities

Snapchat has different functionalities that make it what it is. We will be going through these functionalities and delving deeper into the features we mentioned in Chapter 1.

Before we look at those, let us look at the lingo around the app.

I have used some terms in the previous chapter that you may be unfamiliar with. Or maybe you have heard them used before and you have no idea what they mean. Here are some of them and their meanings in easier terms:

- **Snap**: This is a photo or video that you send with the app. So, you can take a snap and post it on your Snapchat.

- **Snap code**: This is a special marking like a QR code that a smartphone can read. It is a way to have people follow you easily by pointing their phone over yours when it is open on your profile. Every Snapchat user has a unique code that they use.

- **Story**: The Snapchat story refers to a snap that you share publicly for access by all of your Snapchat friends. You can keep adding snaps to your story over 24 hours to share with those who follow you.

- **Friends**: Snapchat friends are those who follow you on the app, that is those who have added you to their Snapchat. They can follow you without you following them back and will still be able to view the public snaps you post.

- **Filters**: These let you change how a photo or video appears. You can do quite a lot with the filters, add information to your snaps to give them more context, or change them up so they look unique and exciting for the viewer.

These are some of the words that you will hear of and that may help you in your marketing endeavor. With that information, we can move on to how Snapchat actually works.

1. Starting out

To begin with, you will need to head on to Google Play Store for Android or the App Store for iOS and download the app. Next is to sign up and create your account, follow the prompts to sign up, and set up your account.

You should choose a username that suits you. For a business, you can have the company name as your user name. The name you choose will be your handle and that is how people will find you on Snapchat, using the name you choose. Be very keen while choosing a handle, as it can't be changed later.

Once you have set up your account, you will then need to add friends. You can do this manually or let the app access your contact list and have all of those with the app in a list so you can choose easily who to add.

Consider adding your previous clients, and any other potential client in your contact list. To add a person, just click on the plus icon beside their name.

1. **Taking Snaps**

Opening the app takes you to the camera screen where you can proceed to take photos. Focus your camera on what you would like to capture and tap on the circle that appears at the bottom on your screen. Holding that circle for longer will prompt the app to start recording a video.

There is the icon on the lower left corner of your phone that shows a downward facing arrow. Tapping on that after capturing your photo will save the image to your phone's gallery and you can view it later.

To add a caption to your snap, tap the icon 'T' and write what you would like. You can zoom and change the position so that it is where you prefer it.

There is a timer icon on the lower left side of your screen. This you can tap on to set the time limit for an image. The time you set is the amount of time one will be able to view the image for.

2. Sending Snaps

You can also send the photo and share it with another user or to the public. Remember that when you send the photo, you cannot retrieve it once more. If you would like to have the photo for future viewing, do not forget to save it first.

Send the image by tapping on the icon at the lower right side of the screen, which is an arrow icon. Select who you would like to share your image with then tap on the arrow button again to send.

3. Accessing Content

You can access different content from other users from the app. To see such content, swipe right. This brings you to the friends' screen.

You can access content they have shared from here. This is of course a more personal front that may not be in your interest as much.

If your main goal is to use the app for marketing, seeing more social posts may not be of benefit to you. There is the option of a more professional front that you can access by swiping left. This takes you to a discover screen where you will find content that is more professional.

Find content from other brands and stories that are popular.

This is a great way to have only content that interests you. You can know about upcoming trends and find what people like, which you can then transfer to your own account and get better results. Stay up-to-date with the world of Snapchat.

4. Changing Filters

Once you have taken a picture, you can change the filters quite easily by swiping left or right. The filter will appear on your image and you can choose which looks best.

You can also add a second filter once you have applied one. Simply press and hold the screen while simultaneously swiping left or right on the screen with another finger.

There are several filters available, for instance, if you want your image to appear in a blue hue or give it a more retro feel you will get just those effects. You can also have filters that show location, though they are only available in specific areas, or times.

5. Altering Videos

You can alter videos you share on Snapchat. The app lets you fast-forward the video, make it slower, or even rewind it. These options may make your video more interesting for the audience and would have more of them watching it.

To apply the options, you first record your video and then swipe left or right to get access to them. There are several icons to guide you to the different actions.

The snail icon is for the slow-motion action and will have your video playing at a very slow pace.

The rabbit icon stands for fast forward, it makes

everything happen a bit faster in the video.

To rewind, you have an arrow that faces backwards. This makes things happen in reverse. For instance, if it was a ball you threw upwards, it will now play in rewind, showing the ball going back into your hands.

6. Snapchat Emoji

There are emojis featured by Snapchat that are only available to you as a user. They usually appear beside the names of your friends. There is the smiling emoji, smirk, sunglasses, and fire, amongst others.

The emoji usually point to different levels of engagement between you and your Snapchat friends. For instance, the smirk shows one who snaps you frequently although you do not snap them that much.

For a business account, these may not apply to you as much as that with a more personal account. However, you can use it to promote interaction, by recognizing the people who are constantly snapping you, encouraging people to give feedback there, and holding contests.

7. Snapchat Stories

These are quite different from snaps sent to individuals. Individual snaps usually disappear after a few seconds of watching them. Snapchat stories on the other hand tend to stay longer than the few seconds.

To post a Snapchat story you can tap on the icon that appears as a square with a plus sign and capture the image or video you would like to share. Alternatively, you can tap on the arrow icon at the bottom left corner of your screen after taking the image, then press on 'My Story' at the top. This adds the photo or video to your feed.

Snapchat stories can be many photos that you post throughout the day. These are great for when you are promoting an event and you can have a series of photos and videos showing behind the scenes, have the audience know about the preparations to get them excited about the event.

The stories usually stay for 24 hours after which they vanish. The viewers can see the stories as many times as they want until the 24 hours are over, after which they will disappear.

While creating content to share on your feed, ensure that you are confident of it. You can have several tries and share only the one that looks best. The content will be there for 24 hours so make sure that it doesn't show your brand in a negative manner.

8. Snapchat Lenses

This happens to be a most exciting feature for most Snapchat users. The feature places a virtual mask on your face when you take a photo. There are several lenses and you have probably seen them.

Those images where the person has a large flower crown on their head, or a pair of spectacles, large rabbit ears on top of their head, a mustache. There are very many lenses that can be used, and Snapchat users love them. They make the app fun to use, and one can spend hours playing around with them.

Since you want to be appealing to the viewers, you can consider using these lenses to make your feed more exciting for them. Add one of the lenses while posting information on the app.

To use them, first, open the app and have the front-facing camera pointed at you such that you can see your face. Tap on your face and hold. The app will detect your face; you will see a mesh outlining the features in your face. Release your hold then.

Once the mesh appears, there should be several lenses that appear at the side of your capture button. These are small circle icons and you can slide through them to see the different effects and choose one that you like.

You can take photos and record videos with the

virtual masks on. They can change your face as well as the environment of your photo. Save the images and share them with your Snapchat friends.

9. Travel Mode

Snapchat can be very annoying in terms of data usage and battery drainage. It uses quite a lot of data and battery when it is running. Your device's battery may drain faster with the app running. To avoid this problem, Snapchat has a feature that takes care of this issue.

Travel mode increases your battery life, and it is an inbuilt feature of Snapchat. Once you turn it on, it stops the automatic downloading of images and videos when you open the app. You can, therefore, conserve data and battery. When you set your app to travel mode, you will choose the snaps to load, and which ones not to.

To change to the travel mode setting, open your app, tap on the ghost icon which appears at the top center of the screen. You will see a gear icon which you should then tap. Turn on the travel mode setting and you are good to go.

These are some of the functions of Snapchat that will give you an easier time navigating through the app, and not getting lost in it. It is quite easy once you get the hang of it. Try it out and use the different features to get the best out of it. Digitize your marketing and get with the times.

How to Use Snapchat for Marketing and to Earn Money

There are about 200 million monthly active Snapchat users. Amongst those users, a total of approximately 700 million photos and videos are sent on a daily basis, with 500 million views per day.

These numbers point to the potential audience for any person interested in using the app, and more importantly, for one who would like to increase their reach.

I know it may be exhausting to think of yet

another social media site to add to your list of sites where you are already marketing your products. Yet these numbers and the possibility they present cannot be ignored.

It is wise to use any platform which provides new ways to connect with your audience of potential clients and those who are already clients of your business. Such statistics are appealing enough to have you looking into the possibility.

Furthermore, we know that Snapchat is different from the other sites, making it stand out more. The strategies placed would, therefore, be different, as well as the audience and their expectations. Depending on your strategy, this can be a blessing or a disadvantage.

Snapchat with its reach and the sort of audience it provides becomes a necessity in marketing strategies. Although it is mostly used for personal gain, the app can indeed be used in business, and could very well earn you money and market your brand.

The audience

Instagram provides a very appealing audience. The demographics of its users are very interesting, as we see that a huge percentage that is over half of the total users of the app are 13-34-year-olds in the US with access to smartphones.

The audience that Snapchat provides is a younger audience. Most of the users are under 25 years old. Your target audience should guide you in your marketing strategy. If you are trying to get the 'millennials' then Snapchat will work wonderfully for you.

Marketing on Snapchat

Snapchat is different from other social media sites. This means that you cannot use the same strategy you use for other sites on this platform. You will need to get new strategies tailored specifically for this app.

Remember that for Snapchat, you are only sharing images and videos with other specific users and having users share images and videos with you. There is no social proof, as you cannot hold onto communication, or have other people commenting on a post you put there a week ago.

With this app, it is all about getting your content to people who will actually engage with it. Getting more people to engage with new content every day is your goal, thus you want to strategize with this notion in mind.

There are techniques that have been used and been seen to work for other businesses that have marketed on the same platform previously. These still continue to work to date. They include:

1. Influencer Marketing

Very popular people who use Snapchat like celebrities tend to have a lot of influence on other Snapchat users.

Take the example of a certain celebrity who posted negative thoughts on Snapchat after it had changed some of its features, and they lost billions of cash due to the ripple effect it had.

Influencers can be a big part of marketing and make quite an impact. You will need to partner with an influencer to grow your following and increase your sales.

To team up with influencers, you will first need to find influencers that align with your brand and then work with them in your campaign. The influencers can work in several ways, and you can choose one or all depending on what you think will work best for you.

a) Full Takeover

This sort of path is where the influencer literally takes over your Snapchat account for a specified amount of time, like for a day or half a day and posts snaps on the account.

To make this method work, you will need to do a lot of advertising beforehand on all other networks and Snapchat itself.

The advertisements will be centered on

informing your followers of the influencer takeover and creating excitement in them so that on the set day they are all anticipating the campaign. Get your influencer to advertise the takeover to bring some of their followers on board too.

This sort of move is best suited when there is an event, and you can have the influencer posting snaps of themselves and other people at your event.

For instance, if you have an open day where people know more about your product, you can have a local popular musician who will entertain people on the day of the event. The musician will post snaps on your account prior to the event showing the activities happening behind the scenes in preparation for the day.

Such would have people talking about the day and may result in you getting a larger turn out and hopefully translating to more sales at the end of the day as well as in future.

You will need to have spoken to the influencer beforehand concerning the kind of content they can share using your account. Make sure throughout the campaign your brand and products are featured. You can even have discounts for the day on specific items.

You may also consider having the takeovers become a frequent thing such as once every other week, where you can have different influencers taking over your account. This would keep your account fresh and exciting and also have you reaching different social circles through the influencers.

This method does have its disadvantages; for instance, you are limited only to the audience you already have in the form of your followers. You can only do so much as to have the influencer hype the takeover to their followers, and that may not yield the best results.

a) Sponsored Posts

This method is generally better than the total

takeover and takes care of the problem of having a limited audience.

In this particular method, you have the influencers you partner with advertising your content on their own accounts.

Once you have identified the influencers whose audience fit your target market, reach out to them and propose your partnering idea to them. You can then work with the influencers to come up with sponsored content to share on their accounts.

You will need to part with some cash for influencer marketing, but because posts only last 24 hours on Snapchat, will not pay as much as other social media sites like Instagram or Facebook.

The sponsored posts should be natural not forced. Including the influencer in coming up with the content should be best. It will allow them to give opinions on what is more natural for them.

However, do make sure that the influencer appears on the image or video. This increases the connection between the influencer and your brand.

Other than having the influencer with your product, also include written content that they should add to further promote your brand and product.

Think of having a discount code as well for your influencer. This would have their followers being more receptive to the idea of purchasing your product.

If you have different influencers over time, having a discount code also allows you to keep track of how good the individual influencers are doing by relying on sales made through the promotion codes. Such information is important to your future strategies as you would know who to go with a second and third time.

Take note that influencer campaigns do not always result in immediate sales. However, having the popular person promoting your content does increase chances for their followers to notice your brand. They will consider your brand while making future purchasing decisions.

Remember, they may not always be in immediate need of what you offer but might later on.

Something as simple as a sponsored shout out to your brand by an influencer may be good for marketing and will not cost you much in case you are working on a very limited budget.

1. Create Anticipation

Snapchat is especially good for showing behind the scenes preparations for a big event. It generally does not require professional, tasteful photos as even unedited images and videos can be shared. With this, you can create excitement using the app amongst your followers and other users.

Post sneak peeks of the event beforehand. Release short videos that end in cliffhangers to have the viewers wanting to attend the event and see first-hand what happens. Use your snaps to tell a story in preparation for the main event.

Use phrases and content that will have the viewers wanting more. You can use phrases like 'Just wait for the ultimate surprise we have in store.' You can even start a count-down in the days leading up to the main event to create even more anticipation.

2. Constant Interaction

You need to maintain a constant interaction with your followers by sharing images and videos daily without fail. What this does is that it puts your brand in the followers' minds, and they have less chance of forgetting your brand if they see it any time they access the app.

You can use these daily snaps to give further information on your products, have their day-to-day use illustrated in short videos. For the daily content, you can also have different features, new product introductions, behind the scenes videos, and videos on the need for the products you provide.

Use Snapchat editing tools to your advantage to come up with fun, engaging content for your followers.

This comes in handy when used with other strategies aimed at increasing your following, such as influencer marketing. Use them together to get new followers and keep the ones you have interested.

Create familiarity to your business for the followers so that they will think of your brand first when in need of a product that you have.

3. Snapchat Promotions

The main aim of this strategy is to increase e-commerce sales. It is best when you have a substantial following as you will be able to have a wider reach.

With these promotions, you can have special coupon codes and discounts on some days that are exclusive to Snapchat followers. You can advertise the coupon codes prior to release on other social networks to have more people knowing of the offers and increase your following that way.

To share the promotion code, first, post a photo or video to your story of your brand or the product you are promoting together with the code as well as a link to your website.

Next, have your audience screenshot the snap and share to their stories as well. Give the code to the users who snap to their story.

You can also encourage your followers to post images and videos of them using your product to get discounts on the product. This particular move would enable you to access user-generated content which works well for marketing and will increase interaction between you and your audience.

Coupon codes allow you to get content that you can share later through user-generated content.

They also create a sense of urgency for users as they feel the need to make a quick purchase before the offer expires.

Maximize on this urgency by reminding the viewers the amount of time remaining before the coupon expires. You can have one day coupons or those for a few hours or days.

The coupon codes are also trackable, which means that you can be able to track the number of people who make purchases or respond to your offer. You can then use this information to plan future campaigns and tweak your promotions accordingly.

Being trackable makes coupon codes very important for you to know just how well your Snapchat marketing techniques are doing. Tracking the metrics on Snapchat may be hard so the codes would help in that sector.

4. Use Geofilter

Snapchat now lets its users purchase a Snapchat

filter and customize it and make it available for other users for a while.

The strategy is especially important to market an event and build hype around it. When you have an event that you are going to host, you can encourage your followers to make use of the geofilter. Have them take snaps with the geofilter promoting your event and share them on their stories.

Post the event on your social media as well as information on the geofilter. Remember that people need to actually know about it so that they can search for it. Do not waste your resources by purchasing a geofilter that no one knows about.

Once you create awareness of the geofilter, Snapchat users should start looking for and use the geofilter. This would have even more people knowing of the event, which would have more people showing up to the event.

Geofilter may also be great for spreading news of your new business if you are just starting one. It will grow your business as it gives you access to people's friends and family, and you have the added advantage of trust between the one who shares a snap and friends.

They should be more receptive of new products than if you were to promote to them directly.

You can ask the viewers who use the geofilter to add information in terms of your link or your handle in their text captions. This will make it easier to find your business for interested parties.

Quick tips

- Use your Snapcode: Have people using your Snapcode to add more followers. They can take screenshots and share with friends, or you can avail it at events to encourage a larger following.

- Cross-Promoting: You should remember to promote your brand across all other networks like YouTube, Facebook, Instagram, and any other you are in.

- Be persistent. Snapchat marketing needs patience and persistence to work. It takes time, and you may not see the fruits the minute you start out on it, yet with time and effort, it will take shape.

- Use Snapchat to test content before having the content on other platforms where the content will remain permanently. Post part of a video you plan to post on your YouTube channel to see the reaction it elicits.

Once you get the hang of it, Snapchat can be quite helpful to your business and actually easy to maneuver around. Of course, it is not for every type of business, but if you understand your business and more importantly your target market, then you should be able to know whether it will work for you.

Experiment with different strategies and techniques, try out new ideas, and do not be afraid to think out of the box. The best thing about the app is its casual nature which calls for less sophisticated content. As long as your content is able to connect with your followers, you are good to go.

Conclusion

I want to thank you and congratulate you for downloading and reading this book.

This book has surely offered you the proven steps and strategies on how to be the best at digital marketing, far from explaining the different methods as well.

This book has taught you all about internet marketing and it is now time to put what you have read into practice for you to find your cheese within the maze.

Go ahead and find your cheese!

www.ingramcontent.com/pod-product-compliance
Lightning Source LLC
Chambersburg PA
CBHW030504210326
41597CB00013B/791